Beliefs, Emotions

and the

Creation of Reality

BELIEFS, EMOTIONS
and the
CREATION *of* REALITY

New Teachings from Jesus

GINA LAKE

Endless Satsang Foundation

www.RadicalHappiness.com

Cover photographs:
© ponytail1414 /Dreamstime.com
© Caleb Knipp /Dreamstime.com

ISBN: 978-1499276961

Copyright © 2014 by Gina Lake

All rights reserved. No part of this book may be used or reproduced by any means, graphic, electronic, or mechanical, including photocopying, recording, taping, or by any information storage retrieval system without the written permission of the publisher except in the case of brief quotations embodied in critical articles and reviews.

Contents

Introduction	vii
1. The Illusory Reality	1
2. The Ego's Reality	23
3. How Beliefs About Yourself Affect Your Reality	43
4. How Beliefs About Others Affect Your Reality	75
5. The Past, the Future, and Now	93
6. A Belief That Takes You Beyond Beliefs	113
About the Author	121

Introduction

That people's beliefs affect their internal reality is obvious and indisputable: Beliefs create feelings, which create an internal emotional environment. What is less obvious is how beliefs affect one's external reality, or the circumstances people find themselves in, which often seem to have little to do with what one believes and feels.

Most people are not aware of the connection between their internal reality (their beliefs and feelings) and what comes into their life. They assume that their inner and outer experiences are unrelated, when they are not. This presumption leads to a false perception of reality. The remedy is to see reality more truly—as it really is, not as the mind assumes it to be.

We are going to explore the exciting arena of creation—how each of you is a creator of your life, or more accurately a co-creator and shaper of it. This act of creation begins with beliefs, is propelled forward by feelings, and is made manifest through actions. Those actions, in turn, cause reactions from others and consequences from life.

The fact that your beliefs create your internal reality and to some extent your external reality is both good news and bad. The good news is that you have the power to be happy because you have the ability to choose what you believe. The bad news is that until you realize that you have this power, your beliefs are likely to make you unhappy, because the beliefs, or conditioning, you were given and those you have acquired along the way largely misrepresent reality. Your beliefs, for the most part, distort and color reality and interfere with experiencing reality as it actually is: You "see through a glass, darkly."

If you are not aware of what you believe and not aware that you have a choice about what you believe, then your life will be shaped by those mistaken and limiting beliefs, and you will be a passive recipient of the results of those beliefs rather than a conscious co-creator of your life. In these pages, we will explore ways of moving beyond any distorted perceptions of reality that may have developed as a result of your beliefs to a truer, clearer, perception of reality.

Each of you has been given and has acquired a set of beliefs that lead to a certain internal and, consequently, external reality. In that sense, you could say that you are programmed with a particular destiny. However, that destiny can be changed and shaped by you once you become more aware of what you are believing and the power you have to believe something else.

Beliefs are potent shapers of reality. It is wise to be aware of this and to become more conscious of what you believe and whether those beliefs are contributing to your happiness and well-being or detracting from that. I am hoping to shed light on this issue so that you are empowered to align with your truest and most fulfilling destiny as a co-creator with the Intelligence behind all life.

As for who "I" am, I am the same "I am" that is within each of you. That was my message when I was alive two thousand years ago, and that is my message to you today. The man you knew as Jesus exists today in the dimension from which I am communicating. However, I am no longer a man or even a human, but spirit, as you are as well and as you will know yourself to be after you leave this earth. From the dimension where I exist, I am guiding the planet and am with all who pray to me, because I so deeply love the human race and the earth.

Please understand that, although you knew me as a man who lived in ancient times, the body and personality I had then was merely a costume, just as your own body is a temporary costume. I am not bound to the persona of Jesus of Nazareth, although I often assume this persona when appearing or speaking to people, to comply with their expectations. I exist with some individuality in this dimension but no set persona or personality. Some may find this heretical, but so be it.

The man you knew as Jesus also exists today within each of you in spirit. The consciousness that is behind all life is no different than your own. They are one and the same. Your being is meant to shine as gloriously as I was said to have shone on resurrection day.

Resurrection is a metaphor for what is possible within every human being. You are divine. This divinity is awakened by realizing the truth that your beliefs are the only thing that keeps you from knowing your divinity. Change or move beyond your beliefs and you will change yourself, your life, and your world.

My purpose is to bring you this very good news: You are divine and, now more than ever before in history, it is possible to realize your divinity, which is to say your loving and peaceful nature. Through simple awareness, inquiry, and a willingness to see the truth, you can become free of all that causes you to suffer and free to create the life you wish to live, which is the life the Father wishes for you as well. You are meant to be happy, and the willingness to explore and expose the false and limiting beliefs that keep you suffering and imprisoned is the key to your divinity and to everything you need to be happy.

I am speaking to you through this author because she has the ability to transmit my words and because she has been devoted to me in many lifetimes as a religious person. However, you do not have to be religious or devoted to me to benefit from these teachings. You simply need to be open to investigating the mystery of who you are.

Jesus, dictated to Gina Lake
May, 2014

Chapter 1

The Illusory Reality

Beliefs create an illusory reality, which becomes one's reality. This illusory reality stands between you and actual reality. Like a pair of colored glasses, this illusory, mind-generated reality changes how reality looks: like clouds, it hides aspects of reality; like a magnifying glass, it magnifies the importance of some things while minimizing the importance of others; and like a fun-house mirror, this illusory reality deceives and makes reality seem scary. Beliefs cause you to perceive things that are not there and to not perceive things that *are* there. Moreover, beliefs cause you to see the world through a singular point of view, the view of "me."

The me that you feel yourself to be is the sense of yourself that is created and upheld by your beliefs. You also have some images, or internal pictures, of yourself, but the sense of you is largely comprised of what you believe yourself to be—beliefs about yourself: "I am this and I am that; I am not this and I am not that. I am someone who likes this and not that."

If you take away all of your beliefs about yourself, you are left with "I am," a simple statement of existence, which is the only absolutely true statement you can make about yourself. If you examine your other beliefs about yourself, you discover that none of them is completely true or true all the time, and therefore none of them is true. Your beliefs about yourself only seem to be true and only seem to be true all the time.

Your beliefs are more like clothing that the "I am" puts on to give it a shape, a definition. This clothing is often necessary to navigate your relationships and activities. You may need to tell someone about yourself: what you do, what you have done, what you like or do not like, or what you want. However, none of these descriptions of or stories about yourself actually defines you or captures who you are, any more than clothing defines a person. Your beliefs give shape to the idea of you and determine how you feel, how you might behave, and what you are likely to do, all of which give further definition to the idea of you. But stripped of all of your beliefs, who or what are you?

When you were born, you were free of all beliefs. You did not even have the concept of "I." You existed as pure being, pure experiencing. You had to learn that you existed separate from your parents and the objects in your environment. You did, however, have many beliefs stored in your unconscious mind from times when you lived before. These unconscious beliefs would be activated and made conscious as you encountered different experiences in this lifetime. But as a baby, your perception was free of beliefs.

As a baby, you saw reality clearly; however, you had no way of organizing and understanding what you saw. As you developed, language gave you a way of organizing the massive amounts of data that your senses delivered to your brain. Language also gave you a way to communicate with others. It allowed you to form relationships, survive, and carry out tasks in the world. What a miracle and gift language is!

And yet, language came at a cost, because with language, came concepts and beliefs. Thus, the sense of "me" was born and the sense of being a separate, vulnerable, struggling entity. With language came the sense of a me in here and everything else out there, and all of the beliefs about "me."

The ego is this sense of being a me. This sense of me is then fleshed out by ideas, or beliefs, about oneself. The sense of self (the ego) dresses itself up in ideas about itself, and a person is born. The person that you think you are is only what you think you are, as there is actually no such thing as a person. What you think of as yourself is only ideas about yourself and a body-mind that seems to be you but which is only a vehicle for who you are. Without beliefs about yourself that define you as a person, you are left simply with am-ness, or beingness, the natural state.

Returning to the natural state, free of the definitions and limitations of beliefs, is what the spiritual journey and human evolution is all about. As an evolved human, unlike a baby, you have a sense of self, which allows you to function independently in the world; however, like a baby, beliefs and self-images don't define you because you know yourself as the am-ness of pure existence. The evolved human being knows himself or herself both as a human being and as divine.

As soon as language develops, beliefs start forming. They are acquired from others and also result from experiences. Beliefs continue to be acquired throughout life and are modified by experience. They can be changed through conscious effort, but most beliefs go unexamined and function behind the scenes as filters and shapers of reality.

These beliefs result in self-images and other definitions of or stories about oneself in relationship to the world as well as countless conclusions about others, the world, God, and life in general. These images and ideas create an illusory reality, which intervenes between you and reality. They become a lens through which you see reality, which distorts and puts a particular spin on reality.

Beliefs create this illusory reality. But it is emotions that flow from the beliefs that make this illusory reality seem real and so convincing. The illusory reality is created by beliefs, but it is strengthened and made believable by feelings.

Emotions, because they are experienced physically and not just mentally as thoughts are, make the belief that caused the emotion seem true and important. Emotions magnify and reinforce the beliefs that gave birth to the emotions and also bring their own level of distortion to the illusory reality created by beliefs.

Emotions distort reality by hijacking one's attention and putting the focus on thoughts and feelings, thereby magnifying the mental and emotional realm and minimizing or leaving out other aspects of reality, such as actual sensory input. While thoughts and feelings are an aspect of reality, they primarily create and sustain your personal illusory reality and do not accurately reflect reality. Thoughts and feelings cause one to get lost in the mental realm and lose awareness of what else is going on and what else is true besides what is being believed.

For instance, if the belief arises, "I don't have enough money," feelings of upset naturally follow. Those feelings make this thought seem true, and you become convinced that you really have a problem—because otherwise, why would you feel so upset? Then you start to feel even more afraid and worried, which makes the "problem" seem all the more real and pressing. So the mind begins to whirl, trying to come up with solutions to your so-called money problem. At this point, you are in a state of consciousness that is not seeing clearly and not noticing the resources you *do* have. You see only what you don't have. You are seeing only half the truth (the half empty glass) and not the whole truth (the partially full glass).

From this contracted, egoic state of consciousness, real solutions are not likely to enter because the state of consciousness that produces solutions is not being accessed. That state would require that you drop all thought, relax, and be in a positive feeling state.

From a contracted state of consciousness, you are also not even questioning the thought, "I don't have enough money." Is this thought even true? Are solutions even necessary? The illusory reality makes a thought seem true, but is it? Where did that thought come from? Whose perspective is it that you don't have enough money? If you buy into that thought, that belief and the feelings it creates will do nothing for you but put you in an unhappy and unproductive state.

What if you didn't believe the thought, "I don't have enough money"? Would you be better or worse off? Does this thought actually serve you or improve your life? Do you need this thought to survive? What does this thought do for you other than drain your time and energy if you believe it? This is the type of examination needed for all of your thoughts.

If you don't buy into that belief or any other, you will simply be present to what needs to be done in your life and you will do it. That state of being present to *everything* that is true in the moment, not just to a belief, is the natural state, and the natural state takes care of itself. If you do not believe that, then examine that belief and those connected to it, because those are the beliefs that keep you tied to the egoic state of consciousness—to the illusory reality created by the ego and other programming.

Taking this example further, if you continue to believe that you don't have enough money and that your mind has the answer to this supposed problem, you will take action in the various directions suggested by your mind: You will get busy doing what your mind suggests you do to solve this so-called problem.

At this point, you may wondering, "What's wrong with that?" That question presumes that answers to how to live your life come from your mind, that is, the thoughts that run through your mind, also aptly described as the voice in your head. If you haven't examined such thoughts, it is natural to believe that the voice in your head has the answers. The thoughts that run through your mind have probably been determining how you feel and what you do your entire life, as such thoughts tend to determine what most people feel and do.

It is wise, however, to examine how well following the advice of your thoughts has worked for you. Has the voice in your head consistently offered good solutions? And do the problems you wrestle with mentally actually exist in reality, or does the voice in your head make them up?

Problems seem to exist, but problems are actually illusory and part of everyone's illusory reality. "Problem" is a concept, not a reality. The mind turns something into a problem by telling you it is a problem. In reality, problems do not exist. You cannot touch, see, hear, smell, or taste a problem or sense it in more subtle ways, because there is nothing there to sense. A problem is imagined.

The most important question to ask in this examination is, "What is the source of my thoughts, and is it trustworthy?" Since there is no answer to where your thoughts come from (you didn't come up with an answer, did you?), then how can you know that your thoughts are trustworthy? Therefore, the only way to know if your thoughts are trustworthy is to examine and question *each* of them.

What is it that is able to examine and question your thoughts? That is a mystery, isn't it? That which is able to examine and question "your" thoughts is the real you. Your thoughts are merely posing as you! Your thoughts are defining a you. However, this is not the real you but an illusory you. Your thoughts create your personal illusory reality, including an illusory sense of yourself and illusory problems. Meanwhile, the you that is able to observe and evaluate your thoughts and see through this illusory reality is who you really are.

The real you uses your intelligence to operate in the world, but it doesn't generally speak to you through the thoughts in your mind. The thoughts that run through your mind day in and day out are the source of your personal illusory reality and your illusory self, the person you think of yourself as, the person who suffers and struggles so with life.

The real you is what is actually alive in you and animating your body-mind. It knows exactly how to keep you safe and unfold your life. The real you speaks to you intuitively and in other subtle ways, not through the commentary in your mind. The real you is also the source of compassion, acceptance, wisdom, peace, contentment, lasting happiness, and love. Every virtue you can name is a quality of your true nature.

Waking up means waking up to the truth about yourself and about reality: You are not who your beliefs tell you that you are, and reality is not what your beliefs tell you that it is. Beliefs stand in the way of experiencing your true self and experiencing reality. Beliefs are all that stand in the way, but that is enough to make this human life a challenge.

To summarize, your beliefs create images (imaginations) and definitions of the person you seem to be, your beliefs define deficiencies and problems that seem to exist, and then the same thing (the voice in your head) that created the illusory self and illusory problems comes up with solutions and advice for how this illusory self should be and move in the world. What a mystery it is to be a human being!

It is no mistake that human beings have a mind that creates an illusory reality, for this allows each person to have experiences that he or she would never otherwise have. Human beings are programmed to create an illusory reality for a purpose: to explore life through a multitude of lenses and to learn and grow from those experiences. An even greater mystery is that you are also divine, and at some point in your evolution, when your personal illusion has begun to dissipate as a result of seeing through it, you discover who you really are, in all your beauty.

The illusory reality's most salient feature is that it has you at the center of it. You are the star in your illusory reality. The beliefs that create your personal illusory reality all relate to you. Even beliefs or thoughts about others are generally in relationship to the me that you imagine yourself to be: how others feel about me or compare to me or are likely to affect me. The thoughts that make up your universe, your personal illusory reality, are in service to the imaginary me. Those thoughts create the me and maintain it. They provide problems for the me to solve, goals for the me to reach, fears for the me to concern itself with, and desires for the me to fulfill.

Whether you are aware of it or not, your mental and emotional world orbits around the me. It may seem like your thoughts are about what you have to do today or what your family needs or what is happening in the world, but the common thread throughout your thoughts is *you*: *your* work, *your* family, *your* world. If your thoughts are focused on others, it is only because you see those people as meaningful in your drama. They are the supporting characters or antagonists in your drama, your movie.

This is not to say that you are selfish and self-centered, only that your thoughts are. This is why one's mental world is ultimately so unsatisfying: It is all about "me." As long as your focus is on the me, you will be constantly searching for satisfaction and fulfillment, because focusing on the me is a place of dissatisfaction and an experience of never having enough and never being good enough.

As you will see in the next chapter, the imaginary me is a set up for unhappiness. As long as you look for the solution to that unhappiness in the answers offered by the voice in your head, you will continue to be unhappy. The unhappiness of the me is only overcome by seeing that the me and its perceptions are illusory and by discovering that there is something else here that has always been satisfied and in love with life just as it is. Until you learn to identify with that mysterious inner joy, you will not be happy, not for long anyway.

This something else that is here is not a better and happier me; it is the experience of no me, of spacious awareness *of* the me and of everything else, with no center, no point of individuation. This spaciousness includes everything and experiences everything as itself. It is the experience of oneself as everything and as nothing at the same time. This is reality stripped bare of all beliefs. This is reality as the mystics know it, and it is reality as you, too, are meant to know it.

Because focusing on the me, the false self, is the source of suffering, striving, and never having enough, once this focus is dropped and you experience yourself as that which is beyond this imaginary me and inclusive of everything, there is great relief, relaxation, peace, contentment, joy, love, awe, wonderment, and fulfillment. This peace and freedom from suffering is the natural state. This is what the me was seeking and, ironically, what the me keeps one from finding. All this was here all along, in reality. Once the illusory reality dissipates, reality shines through, and it is very beautiful.

The spiritual journey is about the gradual and sometimes sudden clearing away of the mistaken beliefs and misperceptions that have interfered with experiencing reality and with experiencing yourself as you truly are. Until some clearing of the illusion has taken place, one's life is focused on the story of "me," "my life," and how the me is doing moment to moment.

The illusory reality created by your mind is much like a movie with you as the central character. That movie tells the story of your trials and tribulations, successes and failures, and ups and downs. In your internal movie, you are not only the central character, but also the narrator and storyteller. Something happens in the saga of you, and a story is told about that: meaning, or spin, is given to that. At every twist and turn, a story is told or a conclusion drawn that relates back to the central character: "That shouldn't have happened (to me), that was wonderful (for me), that was terrible (for me), things always turn out badly (for me), love never lasts (for me), now I will finally be happy, I never get anything right, I've finally made it, nothing will ever be the same, I'm in a slump."

In reality, events happen. Life just happens as it happens. It isn't personal. Who knows why things happen? Life is a mystery that you will never solve no matter how hard you think about it. But the character at the center of the drama gives personal meaning to even the smallest of events, even though there may be no meaning, even though the meaning can never be known.

Stories and conclusions give life a sense of cohesion, and they make life personal—they make life about the central character. These stories, which are based on beliefs and are often themselves beliefs, create a narrative, a storyline. Stories tie together the past, present, and future, giving life a sense of time, which is not inherent in reality. Time, after all, is a mental construct, and mental constructs belong to the mind, not to reality. Only the mind produces concepts and language. Only the mind slices up reality into pieces, labels it, and places it in time.

People's stories not only organize the events in their life into a narrative, those stories also attempt to explain why things are the way they are. Life events are strung together in a story that attempts to explain events or predict outcomes: "That happened because.... When that happens, then...." Such stories are an attempt on the part of the ego to know what it does not and cannot know and to give the character some sense of control over circumstances that are not in one's control. This lack of control over life is very uncomfortable for the ego.

The movie in your head is held together by some kind of plotline: The loser loses, the winner wins, the leader leads, the helper helps. Whatever the character believes himself or herself to be is played out and proven in the story—in life. The character is destined to fulfill that belief.

For example, if your character believes he is fearless, he will be fearless, and that belief will be reinforced. If the character believes she is loving, she will be loving, and that belief will be reinforced. If the character believes he is a criminal, he will commit crimes, and that belief will be reinforced. What the character believes about himself or herself becomes the character's destiny.

Beliefs are more often than not self-fulfilling prophecies. That is why becoming aware of your beliefs is so important. A self-fulfilling prophecy is a belief that is not true but becomes true merely because it is believed.

Here is the way this works: Beliefs shape perception. They cause you to see reality in a particular way by filtering out some aspects of reality, some aspects of your experience, and distorting and magnifying others. This distorted perception—this illusory reality—results in an internal feeling state comprised of interrelated emotions. Those feelings then shape your responses to others and to the world and determine your actions. In turn, those responses and actions provoke responses and reactions from others that tend to reinforce the belief.

For example, take the belief that people are mean. That belief tends to generate an internal climate of anger and defensiveness. Others, sensing and possibly even experiencing these feelings coming from you, are likely to respond coolly to you or with anger. Others mirror back your feelings to you, thereby reinforcing the belief that people are mean.

The perception that people are mean makes it likely that you will notice instances when people are being mean and filter out instances when they are being kind. Or you may assume that people are mean when they are not. Perceptions filter reality in ways that seek to prove one's beliefs. Because the ego has a need to be right, it directs your attention to evidence that supports its beliefs and steers your attention away from evidence that does not support its beliefs.

This creating of reality and learning from what you have created is as it is meant to be. There is no mistake here. Each of you is meant to live out and learn from the beliefs you carry—until a certain point in your evolution when you discover that you have some choice about what you believe and, therefore, about your destiny.

Your beliefs don't have to determine your destiny if you don't want the destiny that your beliefs are creating. You can change your beliefs or detach from and move beyond them. When you change or stop believing your beliefs, your inner reality changes and then external circumstances will follow. You are meant to be *conscious* creators, not just creators. Everyone creates with their beliefs, but gaining control of the creative process by becoming aware of the power of your beliefs changes everything. Your beliefs no longer create your reality—you do, the real you, that is!

Awareness of your beliefs and the power you have to choose what you believe or to believe nothing frees you from your illusory reality and the drama created by your false perceptions. Awareness frees you to create what your heart wants you to create instead of what your thoughts are destined to create. After all, your thoughts have never made you happy for long, but the heart truly does know the way to happiness.

The reason the thoughts that go through your mind do not make you happy is that, for the most part, they come from the ego and unconscious programming, from both this lifetime and others. The ego was not built to generate happiness. Only by learning to detach from the thoughts that run through your mind is lasting happiness found.

When you detach from the voice in your head, all that is left to guide you is the heart. This is not the broken heart that is sung about in love songs but the spiritual heart, the place within the human that receives guidance from its divine nature. This place happens to be located near the physical heart.

The spiritual heart has been guiding you all along, but it is often overshadowed by beliefs. When beliefs stop running your life and the heart takes over, your life will change because you will no longer be caught in your personal illusory reality. You will see all the beliefs and stories that created your illusory reality for what they are, and then you will know reality.

Before closing this chapter about illusory reality, it seems important to define what I mean by reality. Reality is what is left when the stream of thoughts stops or is no longer given attention or prominence. Reality is everything you experience beyond and besides thought and the emotions created by thoughts. This includes:

- ❖ Subtle inner experiences, such as intuitions, insights, wisdom, knowings, inspiration, and drives that come from your true nature;

- ❖ Higher emotions and qualities of your true nature, such as joy, peace, gratitude, love, compassion, contentment, patience, fortitude, acceptance, wonderment, and awe;

- ❖ The experience of oneness and connection with all that is; and

❖ Sensory experience and the energetic impact of sensory experience within one's being.

Reality is the pure *experience* of life without the interference of thought. It is pure experiencing, as babies do, but with the awareness and consciousness of knowing yourself as both an independent entity and as a divine expression of life. This experience is one of unity and completion, fullness and depth of love for all creation, an ability to be human and divine simultaneously, to be divinely human.

This wholeness is what you have come to earth to experience, so when you do experience it, you feel completely satisfied. The end of the journey as a human being is to feel this complete, this unified with all of life. And all that is necessary to finally come home, to this place of peace, is a willingness to see through the illusory reality cast by your mind and also a willingness to be still and be present to what is real and true here and now.

Chapter 2

The Ego's Reality

The beliefs that make up both the personal and collective illusory reality are largely beliefs that the ego holds about reality. The ego's beliefs are easy enough to discover because they appear as thoughts that run through your mind. Your thoughts are primarily your ego's thoughts, along with some conditioning, not really "your" thoughts, not the real you anyway.

This simple fact, that the voice in your head is primarily the ego's voice, explains why most people are the way they are and why the world is the way it is: People think they are what the ego says they are, and people behave the way the ego suggests they behave, at least much of the time. Fortunately, many also respond to the deeper cues that come from their true self.

Interestingly, many of the ego's beliefs about reality are quite different from the truth. The picture the ego paints of reality is not accurate and, consequently, leads to unfortunate results and unnecessary suffering. That suffering eventually wakes people up to reality, so there is method in this seeming madness.

Because the beliefs held by the ego are for the most part contrary to the truth about reality, the egoic state of consciousness, which is the state of consciousness of most of humanity most of the time, could be called insane. To believe and act as if something is true when it is not could be a definition of insanity. It could certainly be called delusional.

However, because most people believe the misperceptions of the ego, these perceptions are not generally questioned, and not without a cost to those who do question them. As in the Hans Christian Andersen story "The Emperor's New Clothes," no one dares to tell the truth to the king for fear of being thought to be stupid. The situation humanity finds itself in is even worse than that: Very few even *know* the truth about reality because most don't think to inquire into the mystery that is life, the mystery at everyone's core.

Fortunately, there have always been those who inquired and who realized the truth and were willing to tell it. And fortunately, times have changed. Questioning is rampant. The insanity of the stream of thoughts that goes through people's minds is being exposed, and people are becoming free from the programming that has kept them in a state of unquestioned suffering.

What is the egoic state of consciousness and what beliefs does it rest on? Everyone knows the egoic state of consciousness well, but it may not be thought of as a state of consciousness if you don't realize that another state is possible. For most people, the egoic state of consciousness seems to be just the way things are, the way life is. For most, the illusory reality created by their thoughts is the only reality, and that reality is scary, untrustworthy, cruel, harsh, and unfair. This is the ego's view of reality, and a case can be made for this. However, the ego is ignoring how abundant and supportive reality—life—is.

Why human beings are given an ego that has such perceptions is a subject for another time.

Suffice it to say that the programming that is the ego is not a mistake but part of the divine design. The ego not only shapes the sense of individuality, it is also behind the drama in life by creating the inner and outer conflict that drives life forward and provides innumerable lessons, which would not occur without this programming.

Reality only seems scary, untrustworthy, cruel, harsh, and unfair because believing that life is scary, untrustworthy, cruel, harsh, and unfair keeps people from experiencing reality as supportive and trustworthy, although reality is admittedly unpredictable and difficult at times. The belief that reality is scary, untrustworthy, cruel, harsh, and unfair becomes a self-fulfilling prophecy.

Those beliefs become the lens through which people see reality. This lens is the egoic state of consciousness, the illusory reality created by the ego. The feelings created by these beliefs, particularly fear and anger, make the ego's perceptions seem true, and then actions (or no actions) are taken in keeping with these perceptions. These actions evoke responses from people and life in general that reflect back and reinforce the internal state of fear, anger, and distrust.

For example, if you believe that life is scary, untrustworthy, cruel, harsh, and unfair, then you may also conclude that your attitude must be "eat or be eaten, attack or be attacked, look out for #1." If this is what you believe, then the aggressive internal climate created by those beliefs will cause you to behave accordingly. And if that is how you behave, then that's how other people are likely to behave toward you. Then that will become your experience and the experience of anyone else who takes on those same beliefs, which they will if they encounter enough people like you.

This is how a particular state of consciousness can come to pervade a world. One's state of consciousness is contagious: Others start to behave toward you as you behave. If enough people are behaving similarly, the beliefs underlying that state of consciousness are reinforced and become more believable, and the illusory reality created by those beliefs appears true and real. Egoic beliefs and behavior create a world where people behave egoically. Beliefs manifest as reality. This is why nothing short of a change in consciousness will change your world fundamentally. This change of consciousness is imperative now.

That consciousness is contagious is also good news. Changing the consciousness of a relatively few number of people can cause a snowballing effect, because the truth has an advantage over the ego's lies, since the ego's lies lead only to suffering and the truth to the opposite. Once enough people see the falseness of their thoughts and realize that their thoughts are the cause of their suffering, and once people realize the possibility of a better reality, consciousness can change quite rapidly.

Much of what keeps the ego's lies in place now is the fear of being different from the crowd, of stepping beyond convention and going against how most people think. Once there is less of a stigma around questioning your programming, because more people are not drinking the ego's Kool-Aid, people will awaken to the truth—to reality—much more easily. You are in the midst of and a witness to a revolution of consciousness, right now, in your time.

Here is another example of how the egoic state of consciousness can become a self-fulfilling prophesy: If you believe that life is scary, untrustworthy, cruel, harsh, and unfair, instead of feeling angry and aggressive, you may feel defeated, powerless, and afraid to face life. Many who find themselves in the grip of addictions feel just this way.

Such an emotional climate makes it difficult to summon the confidence, optimism, courage, fortitude, insight, and perseverance necessary to achieve a happy, fulfilling life. Without the necessary internal emotional climate, you are not as likely to go after what will help you to be happy, grow, have healthy relationships, develop your talents, or do what makes your heart sing. You will probably settle for a life of "getting by," one that seems safe but is unfulfilling and joyless, thereby reinforcing the perception that life is unfair and harsh, and happiness is out of reach.

The life that your ego would have you create, as reflected in the thoughts that go through your mind, and the life that your heart, or soul, would have you create are very different lives. Most people follow their heart at least some of the time if they are at all happy. But many do not, and a life of doing only what your thoughts tell you to do is hardly worth living.

You are here for a reason, and that reason is discovered by following your heart, by following your intuition and your joy, not by following the voice in your head. Isn't it amazing that this is not taught to children at an early age and taught in schools? Instead, institutions teach the opposite: Your mind has all the answers.

The stream of thoughts in your mind is not the same thing as your intellect. Unlike the voice in your head, your intellect does not speak to you mentally but is a tool for performing the mental tasks necessary for surviving, creating, and flourishing.

The voice in your head does not have the answers for how to live your life, although it pretends to. For guidance about how to live your life, you need contact with your true nature, your heart, and attunement to your intuition and other subtle means the soul uses to guide each person. Your mind is not who you are. You are a spiritual being. Your mind, including your intellect, was never meant to be the master but the servant of who you really are.

There is so much about reality that the ego does not include in its perceptions and does not understand, making the ego a particularly poor guide to life. The ego's view of reality filters out the spiritual side of life because the ego does not, and will never, understand the great mystery that is life.

When something leaves so much of the truth out, it is difficult to call it anything but a lie. Partial truths just are not true, although something that is partly true may seem true, which is why the ego's perspective on reality does seem credible.

The ego's limited view of reality also seems true because human beings are programmed to believe their thoughts. You naturally believe what you think. You naturally identify the thoughts that run through your mind as "your" thoughts. And being egocentric, as the ego is, you naturally assume that your thoughts are the correct ones, not just for you but for others as well. This egocentricity and undying trust in the voice in your head makes you feel like you know more than you actually know.

The basic stance of the ego and of the mind is, "I know this because I think this." This self-certainty keeps people from looking more objectively at their thoughts and questioning them. If they did, the illusory reality spun by the mind would fall apart. And so it does, once you start taking a good look at the stream of thoughts that seems to be yours.

The ego's illusory reality is one in which the ego believes it knows, while reality is the experience of mostly not knowing, until you do actually know something. What a difference this is! The ego pretends to know things it doesn't actually know just to feel safe, secure, and right. But how safe and secure does it make you to believe that you know something when you don't? The only security that pretending to know brings is a false sense of security.

The ego, as reflected in the stream of thoughts that seems to be yours, pretends to know what is going to happen, pretends to know why things happened, pretends to know what others are thinking and feeling, pretends to know what others are like, pretends to know what is right for others and for itself, and pretends to have answers and knowledge it doesn't have. That is a lot of pretending, all to avoid the painful (for the ego) truth that the me doesn't actually know very much.

The truth about your moment-to-moment reality is that you don't know very much, not nearly as much as you would like to know. Does that make life scary, untrustworthy, cruel, harsh, and unfair? Only to the ego. Only if you believe it does. Not knowing is just what it is like to live in reality instead of in one's illusory reality.

Not knowing something doesn't feel dangerous or scary once you realize that life operates on a need-to-know basis: You don't need to know until you do, and then you do. It is mostly because the ego doesn't trust life that the ego feels it needs to know. When you trust life, you discover that you don't need to know the things the ego wanted to know.

All of that knowing and pretending to know only gets in the way of purely experiencing the here and now, because if you think you know something about what you are experiencing, you will be mentally comparing your ideas with what you are experiencing rather than just experiencing whatever you are experiencing.

For instance, if you think you know someone, then your image of that person will interfere with experiencing that person freshly and clearly, as he or she actually is in that moment. This bringing of the past and other ideas about someone into your current interactions is the cause of most relationship difficulties. Or if you think you know a flower because you know its name or something about it, you will be busy with your thoughts about the flower rather than experiencing the flower. Thinking and experiencing are two very different experiences, different states of consciousness, really. One is a mental experience and one is an actual experience of reality.

When you do examine your thoughts, you discover that they have a dim view of life, of yourself, and of others. The view from the vantage point of the ego is not only fearful, distrustful, and competitive, but one of scarcity and lack: Everywhere the ego looks, it finds lack. When you look out at the world through your ego's eyes, you see and feel that something is missing: in you, in others, in life, and in your experience. You are not enough, others are not enough, life is not enough, and you don't have enough. This sense of lack and never having enough permeates the egoic state of consciousness. The ego is a programmed, ongoing sense of lack, which imagines lack where there is none.

This programmed feeling of lack is one of the reasons people drink, do drugs, overeat, and try to escape reality in other ways. They are trying to escape the ego's painful illusory reality—and who can blame them? They are trying to escape the sense of not being or having enough by filling the imaginary void within themselves with alcohol, drugs, food, sex, and material things. The trouble is, imaginary voids cannot be filled, because they are imaginary.

This egoic sense of lack creates a feeling of having a problem that needs to be fixed, which the ego is glad to offer advice about. The thoughts in your mind send you here and there, trying to fix a problem that only exists in your mind. The fact that other people's minds might agree that you have a problem doesn't make an imaginary problem real, but their agreement does make imaginary problems *seem* real.

The perception of a problem and desires that stem from that problem as well as other egoic desires drive people's activities and make the world as you know it what it is. Everyone is busy trying to fix their perceived problems and trying to get what they believe they lack and therefore what they believe they need to be safe and happy. This sense of lack drives the greed that has been so damaging to many and to the earth.

When you are no longer in the egoic state of consciousness and the ego is no longer driving you, life naturally unfolds. Part of this unfolding is that so-called problems become resolved and needs and desires get met, and if they don't, you discover that you have the inner and outer resources to deal with that. If you don't take on the ego's view of reality, life will still happen, you will still do things, and you will be safe and okay. In fact, if you stop seeing reality through the eyes of the ego, you will stop feeling unsafe and not okay, and you will start feeling genuinely happy and at peace.

Once you have dropped out of the egoic state of consciousness, you experience security, okayness, peace, love, joy, and the insight and wisdom you need to move safely, effectively, and happily in the world. You don't turn to the voice in your head to define you, define your problems, solve those problems, or steer you toward happiness. From your natural state of being, the experience is one of addressing whatever needs addressing moment to moment, of life flowing and unfolding organically, and of life naturally taking care of itself.

The idea that life takes care of itself sounds absurd to the ego. If this sounds absurd to you, and even if it doesn't, this might be a good place to stop a moment and ask yourself what your mind's objections are to this idea. What arguments or reservations does the voice in your head have when you hear that life is trustworthy and supportive rather than untrustworthy and unsupportive, as your ego supposes?

The Ego's Reality

One of the most common reactions the ego has to the idea that life is trustworthy and supportive is to, metaphorically or not-so-metaphorically, get angry and stomp off. The ego doesn't want to investigate the veracity of its beliefs. It tends to attack and belittle the person who suggests that the ego's viewpoint is a lie. This is a defense mechanism, which helps keep the ego in place. Egos don't question themselves. No real self-examination goes on in the egoic state of consciousness, just "I believe it, therefore it is true." This is how the illusory reality is held in place.

Another response on the part of the ego to the idea that life is trustworthy and supportive might be to list all the ways that life does not seem trustworthy and supportive: "People are starving, people are being shot to death over drugs, the economy is in collapse, terrorists are trying to get us, whole species are dying off, the environment is polluted, there are no jobs, the game is rigged against the little guy, you could die anytime."

The list goes on, without acknowledging that (except for the fact that one could die anytime) so many of the things that make life so nightmarish are created by believing what the ego believes. The ego believes there is not enough, so it takes more for itself than it needs. The ego is afraid, so it grabs for power and abuses it. The ego judges people who are different as bad or inferior and uses that as justification for killing or mistreating them. The ego makes the bottom line—money—more important than the well-being, health, and future of human beings and the planet. The ego's selfishness, egocentricity, and belief in scarcity are behind all manner of tragedy and horror on earth.

In reality, people get sick, they get old, they get injured, and they die, just like every living thing. But this doesn't make life unsupportive or untrustworthy. This is just the way life is on earth. The ego doesn't like death, but there can't be life without death. Death makes room for new life. Reality also gives life, replenishes it when it has been destroyed, and provides what is needed for life to thrive. Reality is bounteous, plentiful, unstoppably alive, and ever new. Reality provides everything you need to exist. The proof of this is that you exist.

Reality is also changeable, unpredictable, and unknowable, but this also does not make reality cruel, unfair, harsh, or even scary or untrustworthy, as the ego concludes. The ego's conclusions are incorrect, an illusion. These conclusions create an inner climate of distrust, fear, anger, powerlessness, and hatred, which manifests in reality in ugly ways and is then mirrored back. Then the ego's belief that life is cruel, harsh, scary, untrustworthy, and unfair becomes a self-fulfilling prophecy. In this way, the ego's illusory reality is created and reinforced.

The truth is that reality is completely trustworthy in its changeableness, unpredictability, and mysteriousness. You can always count on reality changing and changing unpredictably much of the time. Reality is not personally persecuting you by being the way it is; the way it is, is just the way of life.

There is nothing inherently untrustworthy about change or about not being able to know what is going to happen. Reality only seems untrustworthy if you equate unpredictability with being untrustworthy. But that is a misunderstanding. Life is trustworthy *and* unpredictable. But because the ego doesn't like the way life is, the ego believes life is untrustworthy and cruel. Like a child, the ego throws a tantrum because life is not the way the ego wants it to be: "Life shouldn't be this way. Things shouldn't change. People shouldn't die. Life is cruel (because it's not the way I want it to be)."

The person who is afraid of or angry with life, who doesn't trust it and experiences it as cruel, harsh, and unfair is overlooking all the ways that life is supportive. How many times have you been down to your last dollar, when all of a sudden something happened to help you out? How many times have you wondered what you would do next, when an opportunity or idea suddenly arose out of nowhere? How many times have you met just the person you needed to meet or found just the book you needed to read? Everyone's life is full of amazing stories, even seeming miracles, in which life brought something unexpectedly wonderful and exactly what was needed.

When you look for such occasions, you will find them. And many people do. These people are happy. They believe in life. They believe they are partners, co-creators, with something greater than themselves, which is helping shape their life. Life itself is a miracle, and the Intelligence behind life brings you everything you need—and more.

If life is bringing you something you do not want, then that is also what you need. You have to learn to want even that—accept even that—in order to gain from that experience and discover the gift in it.

Limitation is a gift; challenges are a gift. Limitation and challenges hone and shape you and make you stronger. Other people harming you can even be a gift if you don't allow such acts to make you bitter or broken.

Even so, most of the hurt and harm in the world is a result of the egoic state of consciousness. When that state of consciousness is no longer the predominant one on this planet, much of the hurt and harm will disappear, and what will remain is an experience of unadulterated reality.

Chapter 3

How Beliefs About Yourself Affect Your Reality

The beliefs you hold about yourself are powerful shapers of your experience as well as powerful creators and destroyers of possibilities. How you see yourself and what you believe about yourself are very important. And yet, many people are not particularly aware of the effect that their self-images and beliefs have on their lives even though they experience the results of having those self-images and beliefs.

As long as you are unaware of the images and beliefs you hold about yourself, you will be somewhat of a victim of them. I say "victim" because the images and beliefs people have about themselves are often limiting and detrimental, since those images and beliefs are largely determined by the ego and by conditioning.

Self-images and beliefs about yourself are, at the very least, incomplete, and therefore a lie. They misrepresent you because they are only partly true, since they leave out so much. Anything you imagine or think about yourself cannot begin to capture the multifaceted, ever-changing mystery that you are.

Your images and beliefs about yourself are therefore not worthy of shaping your life, and yet, they do. They limit your life—your possibilities. They steer you in a particular direction, which narrows your opportunities and limits what you are likely to experience.

This narrowing of experience is bound to happen. The real question is: Are you living the life you are meant to live, the life that fits for you—for your soul? Do you even *believe* there is such a thing as a soul or a life you are meant to live? If you don't, how does that belief affect you?

If you do believe that there's a life you are meant to live, is it lived by following other people's advice? Or is the life you are meant to live discovered by listening to your own mind? Or to something else?

Do you believe that something else exists to guide you in life besides your thoughts and other people's thoughts? Do you believe there is something called the heart that is meant to guide your life? What does guide your choices? What do you *believe* should be the basis of your choices?

These are very important questions because the answers will determine whether you live according to someone else's ideas, your own, or something else more mysterious, more subtle and yet more real than ideas: your heart.

The trouble with your self-images and beliefs and with following other people's beliefs is that they can cause you to make choices that are not in keeping with your heart, which is the soul's guidance system. Your heart lets you know if your choices are fulfilling your soul's intentions. When they are, you feel joy. When they are not, you feel depressed, unhappy.

If you don't believe this, then chances are you are not following your heart but your ideas and other people's ideas about you. And chances are you aren't happy. The way you know if you are following your heart is whether you are generally happy with your choices. Do you like the life you are living? If the answer is no, your choices probably are not aligned with your heart, or no longer aligned. You are meant to be happy and enthusiastic about life! If you aren't, you probably are not following your heart. And if you aren't following your heart, you are most certainly listening to and believing the thoughts that run through your mind.

People's self-images and beliefs often keep them from doing what they love and creating the life they want and keep them doing what others think they should be doing. This is the source of much unhappiness and depression, which is what living a conditioned life feels like.

People find themselves living a conditioned life, one shaped by other people's ideas or by their own (many of which they acquired from others), because they *believe* they need to please others, or they believe that others know better than they do, or they see themselves as incapable of making good decisions, or they believe they have to obey their parents. And perhaps they don't even believe there is such a thing as guidance from the heart, or they don't trust it. If you find yourself unhappy and living such a life, it can be helpful to answer the following questions:

- ❖ What ideas and beliefs about yourself and about life are behind the choices you've made?

- ❖ What do you imagine yourself to be now and in the future? Is that who you want to be, or is it who someone else wants you to be?

- ❖ If that is not who you want to be or how you want your life to be, then what are you afraid will happen if you no longer had those self-images and beliefs?

- ❖ What would you choose to do if you didn't have those beliefs?

- ❖ What fears might prevent you from doing that?

- ❖ Is it okay for you to go after what makes you happy? Is it okay for you to be happy?

This is a very important investigation. It can make the difference between a happy life and an unhappy one. The only thing that stands in the way of happiness is a thought, a belief. Beliefs can block you from leading the life you are meant to live and they can make you unhappy even when you are living the life you are meant to live.

All of the ideas you hold about yourself come from the ego or are part of the programming that creates the character you are playing in this lifetime. These self-images and ideas give definition to the individual that you are in this lifetime, and that is purposeful. You are here on earth to experience being this character and to learn to create as this character. That act of creation includes creating a life as this character and developing and shaping this character with your choices.

This act of creation is carried out within the parameters you are given, such as your gender, intelligence, culture, talents, and other capabilities. Within those parameters are lots of possibilities, many of which will be untapped by you and which perhaps are meant to be tapped by you, but beliefs stand in the way of you doing so.

You may already be happy with the life you have created and the character you are pretending to be, but if you aren't, you can learn to create something different. You can learn to *be* different, not by pretending to be different or even by affirming that you are different, but different in the most dramatic way—by waking up out of the character you are playing altogether and allowing your true being to be expressed in your life.

When you are no longer allowing your self-images and beliefs to define you and shape your life, then something else much more real comes to the forefront and moves in you to shape your life—but *it* doesn't have a shape. Who you really are has no self-images or beliefs and therefore no psychological baggage preventing it from moving toward possibilities that once seemed impossible or were not even in view.

This that is shapeless, nameless, and faceless has always been present in the background, molding your life to some extent. Once you are aware that that is who you really are, it can play a more prominent role in what you are creating as the character you are playing.

What might this Self, your true self, create? You don't know until you do. This Self moves without the voice in the head telling it what to do. It doesn't need that voice. *You* never needed that voice! This that you really are moves spontaneously, freely, and joyfully as needed and as inspired. A life created in this way is very different from a life that your self-images and beliefs create. With self-images and beliefs, the focus is always on the me: "What do I want, what do I need, and what will be best for me?" Without self-images and beliefs, you respond to what Life wants, what Life needs, and what will be best for Life.

As part of the Whole, you move according to the will of the Whole, the will of the Father, according to Thy will. When you are aligned with your role within the Whole, your life flows, and opportunities and support of all kinds appear. On the other hand, when you believe yourself to be the character that your thoughts describe, then the life you create is the story the character is telling and learning from: If you believe you will never be happy, you will have that experience. If you believe you have to work hard to survive, you will have that experience. If you believe you have to do what others want you to do, you will have that experience. If you believe you won't ever find true love, then you will settle for something else.

This is all well and good and part of everyone's evolution and therefore does serve the Whole in its own way. But creating as this character is a very different level of creation than what is possible. A higher level of creation is possible once you know who you really are and you have learned to create your life from Thy will instead of the will of the character, the will of the ego. Living in accordance with Thy will is a very different experience than exploring the ins and outs of the small will.

At a certain point in your evolution as a spiritual being, you realize that you are meant to create as the being that you are, not just as the ego that you have. The ego and its will, its beliefs, its fears, its desires, and other conditioning create the character that you are playing. This character experiences many difficulties and much suffering, most of which are created by the character's beliefs. As this character, you are learning how powerful your beliefs are, what those beliefs result in, how they create the suffering you experience, and how moving beyond your beliefs can release you from this suffering. So your evolution is centered first on learning how to be a better creator as the character you are playing and then, later, on creating in a more fulfilling way as your true self.

There is much value in learning to be a better creator as the character you are playing. Most spiritual and psychological tools are in service to that. These tools support you in becoming a more effective, kinder, and happier character by helping you overcome mistaken and limiting beliefs and replacing those beliefs with more functional ones. These tools include affirmations, visualizations, positive thinking, hypnotherapy, and the whole range of New Age, New Thought, and more traditional healing technologies.

Becoming a more effective, kinder, and happier character is an important aspect of everyone's growth. You can hardly advance to the next level of creating without working on this level first. Some polishing of the rough edges of this character and diminishing of the negativity in your inner reality is necessary before the diamond at the core of your being begins to shine forth.

Once your illusory reality has thinned and dissipated sufficiently, usually as a result of inner inquiry, emotional healing, and meditation and other spiritual practices, your true being begins to be experienced more strongly and more frequently. Then that begins to move you in your life instead of your beliefs and emotions. Thy will becomes more active in shaping your life, and your life becomes an instrument of creation for Thy will. The personality of the character is still there, but it is put in service to Thy will and becomes an expression of Thy will. Your experience of yourself is no longer as the character but as the being that you are.

Spiritual awakening is marked by this experience of knowing yourself as a spiritual being rather than as the character you appear to be, or that your thoughts would have you be. You become free of the illusory self that is created by your thoughts, your programming.

After awakening, the spiritual being that you are operates as the character you have been playing, for that is the vehicle or costume you have been given, which is necessary for navigating life; however, your being is no longer limited or defined by that character and the thoughts that run through the character's mind. Your being remains empty, spacious, shapeless, nameless, faceless, and genderless, while at the same time appearing as a person with distinct likes and dislikes, talents, and foibles. You are a mysterious blend of human and divine!

In the interest of, first, learning to become a better creator as the character you are playing, let's take a look at some examples of how beliefs about yourself shape your life. First, let's consider beliefs around being a man or woman. Each gender is loaded with beliefs and expectations that shape and limit possibilities, often beyond one's awareness. Every culture has expectations for each gender and so does every family. Children are trained from birth to act a certain way, to develop themselves in certain ways, and to see themselves in a certain way depending on their gender. Meaning is given to gender: "I am a woman/man means...." How you complete this sentence reveals the beliefs you hold around your gender, many of which are limiting.

How has your gender determined your choices and shaped your life? You would undoubtedly have had a very different life if you had been born as the opposite sex and not had the conditioning that came with your gender, but then you would have had the conditioning of the other gender. When it comes to gender, there is no escaping conditioning and some narrowing of options.

And yet, your gender is not a problematic limitation from the standpoint of your soul, since your soul selected your gender because that gender could best serve your lessons and purpose for this lifetime. Gender and the conditioning that comes with it is an example of programming that narrows down options and provides challenges but does not necessarily inhibit the soul's evolution. Rather, your gender is part of the soul's evolution. And yet, you can appreciate how even the imprinting of something as basic as gender can profoundly limit and shape your life.

So not all imprinting and the limitations and challenges it imposes are a problem for the soul and its evolution. However, there is one kind of imprinting that can be very limiting and can inhibit the soul's evolution, and that is the imprint of psychological wounding. This is not to say that emotional wounding might not be part of the soul's plan—grist for the spiritual mill—because it often is. However, emotional wounding is the kind of imprinting that can severely limit one's happiness for lifetimes. So bringing awareness to the beliefs that underpin any emotional wounding is especially important.

Emotional wounding creates the deepest distortions in one's personal illusory reality and therefore the greatest suffering. Emotional wounding takes the form of beliefs about yourself that create enormous pain and limit your possibilities and therefore the potential for a happy and fulfilling life. Emotional wounding keeps you stuck in the lies your mind is producing and marching to the drumbeat of the ego, which is a drumbeat of fear, negativity, and not enough.

Emotional wounding creates a darkly distorted view of yourself and of life, which spreads its poison to others, often through more abuse or destructive acts. In other words, emotional and physical abuse wounds people emotionally, and those emotional wounds lead to either further self-abuse or abuse afflicted on others. Becoming aware of the beliefs behind the emotional wound frees you from this cycle of pain and hurt.

When you are young, you have no identity; you don't know what to think about yourself. Ideas about yourself are given to you by past-life imprinting, parents, siblings, relatives, teachers, friends, and others close to you when you are growing up. You are told who you are, sometimes directly but often covertly and subtly. Children also draw their own conclusions about themselves based on their experiences. One's identity is made up of ideas collected along the way from all of these sources.

The problem is that once these beliefs are formed, they aren't easily reshaped or erased. And once they are established, they tend to become self-fulfilling prophecies, which reinforces those beliefs. Consequently, what a child is told early on about himself or herself is crucial and will largely determine how happy and fulfilled he or she will be. If the messages were negative, that person will have to work to overcome that programming through awareness of it and a conscious attempt to reprogram those ideas. Because the illusion is not that easily seen through, this can take years of diligent effort.

If the programming you received was detrimental and limiting, then that is the spiritual work you have been assigned. You are here to learn how beliefs create reality, and that starts with how your beliefs create the reality you are experiencing. If you received difficult programming, it is not a mistake. It is what your soul signed up for to learn to be a more conscious creator. What better way to learn to do that than to first create something unpleasant? Suffering motivates people to create something better or to make the world a better place.

So much growth is accomplished in the lifetimes when you received detrimental programming. In such lifetimes, it is possible to grow by leaps and bounds, which is why a soul chooses difficult circumstances. Such lifetimes are a crash course in creation. If the learning is not accomplished in that lifetime, the learning continues in between lifetimes and into the next. How long it takes is no problem for the soul.

Let's take the example of the belief "I'm not worthy of happiness." This is a very common belief, although often unconscious. It is a real stopper, because every time you approach feeling happy, your unconscious mind, or the ego, must sabotage that happiness or be proven wrong. Both conscious and unconscious beliefs beg to be proven correct because the ego, which is part of your programming, doesn't like to be wrong. Programming is, after all, programming, and it seeks to maintain itself any way it can.

One of the main ways the programming maintains itself is by filtering out evidence that contradicts the programming. The belief "I'm not worthy of happiness" ensures that you will filter out possibilities for happiness. This might mean that you don't seek out activities or relationships that would make you happy, because if you did, you would prove your programming wrong. Instead, you are likely to engage in relationships and activities, such as addictions, that don't make you happy, thereby fulfilling the edict of your programming. This all happens, of course, unconsciously, as no one purposefully seeks to create circumstances that will cause unhappiness.

The illusion is very tricky, and one reason it is, is that it is generated and maintained unconsciously. For you to see through your personal illusory reality, you have to become aware of the workings of the unconscious mind and of beliefs that were formerly unconscious. You have to become aware of how you, yourself, and nobody else, is creating your experience of reality and to some extent also creating your external reality by believing what you believe.

The place to start in becoming more conscious of what the unconscious mind is up to is to become aware of what you believe—to become aware of the thoughts that run through your mind. Becoming aware of the beliefs that you *are* conscious of is the first step in unearthing unconscious beliefs—because the beliefs that you are aware of are connected to the beliefs that you are not conscious of. When you tug on the string of a conscious belief, it pulls up, from the unconscious mind, beliefs related to it that you were formerly unaware of.

The best way to uncover unconscious beliefs is to practice observing your thoughts, as is done in mindfulness and other types of meditation, and then to dig more deeply into the limiting beliefs that you are aware of through the technique of spiritual inquiry, which this author has written about elsewhere, as have many others.

This investigation is bound to expose some beliefs that you didn't know were there. In this way, a complex of beliefs that uphold each other, including some unconscious ones, is likely to be revealed. Once this complex of beliefs is sufficiently seen as being untrue, those beliefs lose their power to fool you: Once you have seen through an illusion, as in a magic trick, you can no longer be fooled by it.

Let's take another common belief that holds people back: "I'm not lovable." Other ways this belief might be stated are: "Other people don't like me. I don't like myself. I'm not good enough (to be loved)." This belief becomes a self-fulfilling prophecy in the following way: If you don't perceive yourself as lovable or if you don't like yourself, you feel bad inside. You are living in a negative internal climate, which feels heavy, separate from others, sad, and possibly angry and resentful. Envy and jealousy are also probably present at times.

Such a negative emotional climate makes you feel dark, heavy, negative, and needy, like a black hole. It also affects how you appear to others: You don't smile much, you don't make eye contact, and you keep to yourself. It's like being painted black and makes you almost invisible to others.

If you feel this way inside, others are also likely to sense this about you. If others don't pick up on how you feel by how you appear, then how you feel is likely to be revealed by what you say: You may complain, disparage yourself, judge and gossip about others, play the victim, or drain others with your neediness.

You may not think you are self-centered or self-absorbed, but such a negative internal climate keeps you focused on yourself, your needs, your desires, and what you lack. A negative internal climate keeps you spinning around in your illusory mental reality, the ego's world, trying to fix the way you feel, not realizing that the ways the ego comes up with to fix you won't help. Meanwhile, you aren't very aware of what is actually happening in reality, including possible opportunities or any love and support that may be coming your way.

When you are focused on yourself, you aren't able to be present or loving to others or available to help them. If you were, that would be an attractive, not to mention pleasant, state. When you aren't open and loving to others, then you won't be perceived as very likeable. And if you want their love or anything else from them, they often sense this and move away. The prophecy that others don't love you becomes fulfilled, because the you that your internal state has created is not very lovable. And of course, it is also difficult for you to love yourself when you feel this way, no matter how many affirmations you may repeat.

Even when you don't love yourself, you can have compassion for yourself, which is the beginning of loving yourself and getting in touch with your inner light and letting that shine. Compassion for yourself is the bridge that takes you out of the grip of your personal illusory reality into reality, because compassion is a quality of your true nature.

This is a Catch-22, though, isn't it? How do you find compassion for yourself in your inner darkness?

Well, you have to look for it. That's all, really. It *is* there. Compassion is the key. Once you know that it is the key, then feeling loving toward yourself is just a matter of using the key. But that does take a willingness to see the truth about why you don't love yourself and a willingness to use the key.

Here are a few more, simple examples of how beliefs about yourself become self-fulfilling prophecies. If, for example, your self-image is that you don't like to exercise or that you don't like to eat right or that you are someone who adores food, your unconscious mind will do its best to uphold that self-image. One of the ways it does this is through stories: Whenever the subject of exercise or eating comes up, you tell others the story of how you don't like to exercise, how you don't like to eat right, or how much you adore food.

If you don't continue to live up to that image, that will make you wrong, and the ego doesn't like to be wrong. So if someone says, "Want to go on a hike?" You check with your self-image, see that hiking doesn't fit your self-image, and reply, "No thanks. I don't like to hike." Or if someone says, "I feel so much better after changing my diet. You should try it to," you reply, "No thanks. I don't like to eat healthy food" or "I love food too much to do that." Then you continue to live your life in keeping with your self-image: You don't exercise, you don't eat healthy food, or you put food at the center of your universe—because if you didn't, you wouldn't be being true to yourself, true to your self-image. In this way, you become what you believe yourself to be and what you tell others about yourself. By closing off opportunities to experience yourself differently, your beliefs about yourself are proven true and fortified.

Let's look at one more example of a belief about yourself that becomes a self-fulfilling prophecy and limits your possibilities by creating a distorted, illusory personal reality. The belief is "I'm a failure." This belief could be stated in a number of different ways: "I don't believe in myself. I won't succeed at anything I try. I'm not as good as others, so there's no use trying. I always screw up. I'm not like others—nothing I do works. There's no hope for me."

As you can imagine, this is a very debilitating belief. After all, life is made up of moments of doing, or attempting to do, one thing and then another, often something you have never done before. When you believe you are a failure, then everything you do becomes a test of your self-worth. It is painful to take life this personally, and if you believe you are bound for defeat, it would be easy to conclude, "What's the use of living?" And many feel this way.

The belief that you are a failure becomes a self-fulfilling prophecy for a number of reasons. First of all, this belief creates a negative internal climate that not only feels bad to you, but also feels bad to others and makes you appear unattractive to others. A negative internal climate tends to repel people and opportunities that could smooth your way, just as the belief "I'm not lovable" does.

More importantly, the belief that you are a failure undercuts your motivation and saps your energy, because negative emotions are draining. To succeed, you at least have to try, and usually repeatedly—you have to persevere. "If at first you don't succeed, try, try again" is very sound advice. But unfortunately, those who believe they are a failure often don't even try the first time, much less persevere.

At this point, it seems important to note that success actually only exists in the ego's illusory reality, because success is a concept. It isn't real. There is no clear definition of success, and there never will be. If you do achieve success, your ego won't let you rest for long before it redefines success. Then you are chasing after success once again. You never attain it for long. This is not to say that you shouldn't try to be successful at what you do, only that *you* will never *be* a success or achieve it for long, because your ego constantly redefines what that means.

What is important to your soul is evolving by learning, and learning results from so-called failures. Trying and failing, and trying something else and possibly failing, and trying again and succeeding, and then trying something else and failing is how life naturally unfolds on planet Earth. To your soul, failure *is* success, because that is how learning happens!

When you think of yourself as a failure, you are taking life very personally. Failure doesn't exist in reality, any more than success does. "I'm a failure" is the ego taking life personally. With the ego, everything that happens turns into a story about "me," when in reality, what happens is just how life is happening.

The solution to a belief such as "I'm a failure" is not necessarily to affirm the opposite. Affirmations are often not enough to transform deeply embedded unconscious beliefs, which need to come to the surface first before they can be transformed.

Beliefs are transformed by seeing that they aren't true. You may need to see that a belief isn't true many, many times to become free of it, not just once. You need to do this for as long as a feeling, such as the feeling of being a failure, is experienced. If a negative feeling state is there, then beliefs must be there. If you can become aware of the beliefs behind that feeling state and then investigate them until you uncover the unconscious beliefs that are connected to the conscious ones, then that will release you from the grip of those beliefs and feelings. Of course, part of this investigation is seeing that those beliefs are not true.

With beliefs such as "I'm a failure," the question needs to be asked: "Where did this belief come from?" It is in your own mind, but where did it originate? Who or what put it in your mind? Can you find the origin of that belief? If you look, you can't. This is equally true of any belief that you hold about yourself. You cannot find the origin of any of your thoughts.

You might say that your father put that thought there or that you put it there (in which case you should be able to remove it). But the truth is, that thought and lots of other ones are just there. Your father might have told you that you were a failure, but he didn't put that thought in your mind. It's just a thought in your mind, and it must have been a thought in your father's mind if he said that to you. Who or what put that thought in your father's mind?

Where do your thoughts come from? Are your thoughts or anyone else's the truth? Are your thoughts or anyone else's God's thoughts? Do people's minds speak the truth? With even a superficial examination of the voice in your head, it becomes obvious that the voice in your head is not even close to being the voice of God or the truth. The thoughts in your mind are more like the opposite of the truth than the truth. They are more like Satan than like God.

So why would you believe such thoughts? The only reason you do is that you were programmed to believe what seem to be "your" thoughts. But they are not your thoughts. Believing that they are is the foundational lie that makes the illusory reality possible.

Those who are successful already believe they are or can be successful even if they don't appear successful at a particular moment. Believing this keeps them motivated and persisting when things aren't going well. They believe that at some point their efforts will lead to success—who knows when? Those who are successful keep the "when" open, never concluding that they have failed just because they may be having difficulty.

Sometimes the only difference between someone who achieves what he or she sets out to do and someone who doesn't is a "can do" attitude, which you might call hope. Optimism and hope create a positive internal climate, which leaves the door open to possibilities and makes manifesting those possibilities much more likely. This begs the question: How might you have narrowed down your possibilities unnecessarily simply by *believing* something wasn't possible?

It's not that those who are successful are successful all the time. They are likely to have had many experiences of failure, but they don't define those experiences as such or let those experiences become the belief "I'm a failure." They don't take their so-called failures personally. They don't turn an event into a story about themselves. Only the ego—the great saboteur—does that.

Here's how the belief that you are or can be successful becomes a self-fulfilling prophecy: This belief creates a positive internal state, which is attractive to others and attracts opportunities. When you believe in yourself, others believe in you, and they naturally want to help or join with you, which makes success more likely and happiness inevitable even if success is not immediate.

Your internal climate is really important! It is like a signal, or vibration, you send out. Those who resonate with that vibration will be attracted to you, and those who don't resonate with that vibration, won't be attracted to you. This means that if you are broadcasting a vibration of limitation, failure, and self-hate, others who resonate to that sad song will gravitate toward you, while those who dance to a happier tune will be repelled.

People with similar internal climates flock together and sing the same sad—or happy—song together, reinforcing each other's internal realities. People live in different realities: Each person is in his or her own illusory reality, surrounded by many who are experiencing a similar illusory reality. And then there are those who live mostly in reality, who have a much better experience of life.

This explains to some extent how people can have such divergent views of life. For example, some see people in general as mean, while others see people as nice. As a result, some people don't like people, while others love people. Your beliefs create an internal state, and that results in a particular experience of reality—a particular reality.

While a negative internal state is created by spinning around in your thoughts and believing your thoughts, a positive internal state results from simply not being lost in the illusory reality generated by thought. When you are present to reality without thoughts and feelings distorting your experience, your internal state will naturally be positive.

A positive internal state is actually your natural state. Your true nature is content, joyful, loving, compassionate, at peace, and accepting. It is naturally alert to reality and notices and responds to what is actually happening without the usual distortion caused by thoughts and feelings. Your true nature is naturally wise and responsive to life. In any moment, it knows exactly what to do and when to do it.

Not letting your thoughts and feelings interfere with your responses to reality doesn't mean you won't use your rational mind when you need it. It's just that people who achieve what they set out to do don't let their egoic thoughts determine their inner climate. They use their mind for what they need it for, and the rest of the time, they are aware of what is being presented in the moment, what is coming out of the flow. The magic of life happens when you are tuned in to the flow, where it is going, and what your particular role in that is. If you are lost in thoughts and feelings, you won't be in the flow and you won't notice the opportunities that come out of the flow.

Your beliefs are not all that is shaping reality. Your beliefs determine your internal reality and affect how you behave and therefore affect reality to some extent. But something much more mysterious is at the helm of life, and it—Grace, or Thy will—is steering life in a particular direction, which I'm calling the flow.

The flow is the direction that Life is taking, and the flow is not up to you. You do not control the flow, although you influence it in small ways. However, you do determine your *experience* of the flow—of reality—mostly by choosing what you believe and by choosing to either accept what the flow is bringing or rail against it.

When you go with the flow, life feels much easier; when you resist it, life feels especially hard. The egoic state of consciousness is the experience of being upset with the way things are, while the flow is what life feels like when you aren't involved in your ego's beliefs, so-called problems, fears, and likes and dislikes.

Sometimes the flow brings success, and sometimes it brings challenges, roadblocks, or what you might call failure. You are not in control of what the flow brings. However, you are in control of whether you are noticing the flow—whether you are paying attention to reality—or whether you are lost in your mental reality. And, importantly, you are in control of your attitude toward what life brings.

If you can maintain a positive inner climate, that will help you drop into and remain in the flow. Then life will feel much easier and Life's opportunities and support will be more apparent. Doing the work of weeding out or learning to detach from beliefs that create a negative internal climate is so important, since such beliefs are what prevent you from being in the flow and, consequently, from tapping into the wisdom and resources you need to handle whatever the flow is bringing.

Chapter 4

How Beliefs About Others Affect Your Reality

As we have seen, your beliefs about yourself affect how you feel about yourself, how you experience others, and what kinds of people you attract. Your beliefs about others are equally important in determining what kinds of experiences you will have with others and in relationship. The beliefs you hold about those around you determine how you will relate to them and how they will experience you. So let's take a closer look at this great mystery of how you create your experience of others and, consequently, your experience of reality.

Your beliefs about people in general as well as your beliefs about specific people shape your experience of them. As for people in general, what is it you believe? Do you believe people are mean or nice? Do you believe they like you or not? Do you believe they are trustworthy or not?

And, of course, you believe different things about different groups of people: You have beliefs about poor people, beliefs about rich people, beliefs about children, beliefs about teenagers, beliefs about Christians and Jews, beliefs about Americans and every other nationality, beliefs about the different races, beliefs about women, beliefs about men, beliefs about the elderly, beliefs about attractive and unattractive people, beliefs about intelligent and not-so-intelligent people, beliefs about overweight and thin people, and on and on. That's a lot of beliefs to be aware of and examine!

No matter how the mind divides humanity up conceptually, the ego has an opinion about those people, and it believes its own opinions. Do you see how artificial these groupings and boundaries are, how they are made up by the mind? How can opinions about imaginary groups be anything but imaginary—not real, not true?

And isn't it interesting how your mind has an opinion about everyone and every group—instantly! That's what minds do: They form opinions instantly, and you instantly believe your own opinions. Opinions are beliefs, and like beliefs, opinions often go unquestioned and unexamined.

Any of your beliefs can and will shape your behavior toward someone, especially if you are not aware of your beliefs and their effect on you. The more aware you are, the less your beliefs unconsciously shape your behavior. And since beliefs can be especially destructive to relationships, the less your beliefs interfere in your relationships, the better it is for everyone. Unconscious beliefs limit your ability to behave flexibly and respond naturally and freshly to the person in front of you.

Your beliefs limit your choices about how you behave. For instance, if you don't trust men, you will behave as if you don't trust them instead of in the many other ways you might if you did trust them. You won't be free to be more open toward a man, which is more functional than being closed. Being more open and trusting doesn't mean you won't be discriminating and careful, because if you are very present to what is actually happening in the moment, your intuition will let you know if you are safe with someone or not.

The ego's beliefs are its rules for how to live. The trouble is that the ego's rules and formulas don't take into account what is actually happening. Approaching every situation with the same set of rules and formulas is not going to give you very good results; and yet, that is what living according to your beliefs is like. Living this way is like wearing the same clothes every day of the year no matter what the weather is like. Just as you adjust your clothes to the temperature, you have to adjust your behavior to the present moment. If you are living in your illusory reality instead of reality, you won't make those adjustments.

Sometimes men can be trusted and sometimes they can't, to return to our example. The belief that men can't be trusted is untrue because this only applies to some men. A belief that is true only some of the time is hardly going to be useful in guiding your behavior.

The mind loves to lump people in categories. It's simpler that way. It's also just how this primitive aspect of the brain, the ego, works. It sees things as either black or white, good or bad, trustworthy or untrustworthy, with nothing in between, even though even the simplest of things, not to mention human beings, is multifaceted, complex, and mysterious.

Your beliefs about others not only limit your flexibility with others and your ability to be with others freshly in the moment, but also create a particular experience of reality that reinforces your beliefs. Just as beliefs about yourself become self-fulfilling prophecies, so do beliefs about others.

Let's take a look at how the belief that men can't be trusted can become a self-fulfilling prophecy. If you are a woman who doesn't trust men, you will expect men to treat you badly, lie to you, hurt you, or betray you. If you feel this way inside, you will be looking out for yourself in whatever relationship you are in. You will be on guard, and love won't be flowing easily from you to the other person.

If that's the case, then love is not so likely to be flowing toward you either. Or if your partner is expressing love, either you won't be able to receive his love or it won't register. Your filtering system will notice the times he isn't being attentive or the ways he seems untrustworthy, not the ways he is.

Because your ego wants its beliefs upheld, your unconscious mind might even compel you to do and say things that are unkind and cause your partner to withdraw or be unkind in retaliation, without realizing your role in this. If you are unkind, insecure, defensive, or cold in relationship because of some belief, that inner climate is bound to sabotage your chance for a healthy relationship. Who you are likely to end up with is someone who is willing to be with someone who is unloving, insecure, defensive, or cold because he needs to be with someone—anyone—rather than because he loves *you*. This can't be a satisfying relationship for long, and your belief becomes a self-fulfilling prophecy.

Alternately, if you distrust men and therefore expect men to treat you badly, you are likely to accept such a relationship. Here is how that works: If you believe that men treat women badly, but you don't want to be alone, you will accept bad treatment from someone because that will seem normal. When you don't expect anything better from a partner, you will accept the behavior that you expect because you don't expect to find a man who treats you well.

This happens all the time in relationships. If you set the bar low and don't expect to be loved and treated well, you will settle for a relationship that has very little love. On the other hand, if you expect to be loved and treated well, you won't stay with someone who doesn't love you and treat you well. This is how beliefs limit and shape people's relationships.

Your expectations and beliefs can limit possible relationships and cause problems in your relationships in another way: If you require that another person look or be or act a certain way before you will love him or her, you are greatly limiting your chances for love. Finding someone who meets your specific requirements will be difficult, if not impossible. And if you are already in a relationship, your expectations and ideas about how you want your partner to be will only cause conflict between you.

You just can't win with beliefs! Whether your expectations are high or low, they will cause problems, because life is not designed to meet your desires and expectations. Life has its own purpose and its own plan. Life brings you the people it does for many reasons, which you may never understand. Your only choice is whether or not to love who Life brings you.

The mind has its ideas about how relationships should be and how others should behave, but these ideas only create suffering for everyone. Love is possible only when you drop all ideas and beliefs and meet another just as he or she is showing up in the moment, fresh and new. Any ideas you bring into that moment about that person or about anything else will only interfere with experiencing that rich, unique moment with that person.

Love is experienced anytime you are truly present to the person in front of you without any ideas, beliefs, or expectations. Love is not the result of getting someone to fit your ideas or finding someone who does. If you wait for life to fit your beliefs and desires, you will be waiting forever.

Moving beyond your beliefs about others allows you to experience them as they really are. Then it is possible to feel the love that naturally flows between one being and another when beliefs no longer impede that flow. Love is your true nature, and only beliefs stand in the way of experiencing your true nature and someone else's, because beliefs keep you in the ego's illusory reality.

Some beliefs can override or counteract ones that limit or inhibit love. They are beliefs that would come from your true nature if it spoke to you, as the voice in your head does. Such beliefs reflect certain universal principles and truths. Here are a few examples:

You are a unique and precious expression of the Divine. I honor and respect your uniqueness. How you are different from me is a gift and as it is meant to be.

You are lovable just the way you are. You don't need to change for me to love you.

You are not in this world to fulfill my needs or for my purposes but for your own purpose, which I honor and support.

You have your own lessons, and I support you in making your own choices and learning what you need to learn from them.

Any belief or idea that allows love to flow within you and within those you are relating to is a belief that is very close to the truth about life—close to reality—and therefore can be helpful in counteracting the untruths the ego produces.

Some beliefs are truer than others. The closer your beliefs are to the truth about life, the more you will feel the peace, love, joy, gratitude, and contentment of your true nature. A test of how true or useful a belief is, is whether it blocks love or allows love to flow. Beliefs that contribute to the ego's illusory reality interfere with love and make you feel bad and contracted inside, while beliefs that represent life more truly allow love to flow and make you feel good and expansive inside.

The more time you spend in the present moment without your thoughts, the more you are able to know life as it truly is, as your true self experiences it. If you spend enough time being fully present in the moment, you discover the truth about life—that it is good, trustworthy, wondrous, miraculous, and divinely and intelligently guided. Only your personal illusory reality keeps you from realizing this. Your beliefs cause you to misperceive life. Once the lens of your perception is cleared of the beliefs that distort your vision, you can see life as it really is.

Beliefs like those just listed override the ego's erroneous beliefs and take you to the *experience* of the truth. They point to something that is not a belief but rather a universal truth, which when realized, results in peace, love, and harmony within you and in your relationships. That is how you know something is true—because it results in peace, love, and harmony. That is the test. If you apply this test to your beliefs, you will see that not many of them pass the test.

You don't need your beliefs! What a radical idea that is. Your beliefs only get in the way of reality, which is the experience of peace, love, and harmony. That is what reality is! Just that. Reality is the experience of peace, love, and harmony.

Let's delve a little more deeply into how your beliefs about others affect your reality, because seeing the truth about your beliefs frees you from the damage they do to your relationships. Yes, seeing the truth is enough to free you. Nothing more is needed. But there is a lot of examination to be done, since the mind is full of lies and partial truths.

Your beliefs and ideas about the specific people in your life have an enormous impact on your relationship with them—as do their beliefs and ideas about you! More often than not what makes or breaks a relationship are the beliefs and ideas each person has about the other and about the relationship, rather than compatibility or other factors.

If you have positive beliefs and ideas about someone, you will be open to that person, and love will flow easily. But if you have judgments about someone, those will taint your relationship and interfere with seeing the good in that person and with loving him or her. Based on this, you can imagine how many more opportunities for relationship someone who is not judgmental has than someone who is.

Judgments are the number one reason relationships feel difficult, fail, or never get off the ground to start with. And every single one of your judgments is made up by your mind. It wasn't handed down to you from God, because God is the antithesis of judgment, despite how God is sometimes portrayed. Your judgments come from a darker place, a primitive place.

If you are having a problem with someone, you need to examine where the problem lies. Is it in the other person or in your own judgments? Perhaps the problem also lies in the other person's judgments. Without judgments and stories about someone, is there a problem? There may be differences that need to be worked out, but the mind often creates unnecessary problems.

Some important questions to ask about your judgments and beliefs about someone are: "Is this always true or just sometimes true? Is the opposite also sometimes true? Do I really know this about this person or am I assuming this? Am I just pretending to be able to read this person's mind?"

If you investigate your judgments and beliefs, you discover that the mind makes a lot of assumptions and pretends to know things it doesn't actually know. The ego does this because it wants to feel superior and right. It also does this because it loves to tell stories that cause problems and stir up emotions. The ego loves drama, and it doesn't trust love, so it does what it can to sabotage love.

The more important question is: "Is it helpful to the relationship to assume whatever I am assuming?" Judgments come from the ego and are in service to it, so questioning your judgments and their value in general is important. Once you see how useless and damaging judgments are to relationships, you will quickly learn to disregard them.

That judgments close hearts should be pretty obvious. Judgments come from a closed heart, so naturally they also cause others to close their hearts. Judgments are a perfect example of an internal reality, or climate, determining one's external reality. When you openly judge others, you will be judged in return, as predictably as the night follows the day.

Even if you keep your judgments to yourself, the internal climate created by your closed heart will result in others closing their hearts to you, even if they don't know why your heart is closed: Like attracts like, judgment attracts judgment, a closed heart attracts and causes closed hearts, not open ones.

Let's take a look at how the judgment "You don't pay enough attention to me" can become a self-fulfilling prophecy. This judgment, like all judgments, closes the heart, both of the person who holds it and of the person who receives it. The last thing that the person who receives this judgment wants to do is give the person the loving attention he or she is demanding—prophecy fulfilled! Judging someone is a really poor strategy for getting what you want. Judgments backfire every time.

Even if you don't say, "You don't pay enough attention to me," your closed heart, alone, creates the experience of not having enough love. No one else but you can actually make you feel love or feel loved. That is solely up to you. Love is an experience that happens within you. It is an experience of your heart being open. If your heart is open, you won't need love from another person. It's only when your heart is closed that you feel a need for love from another. In holding this judgment, "You don't pay enough attention to me," you create the very experience you are complaining about—a lack of love.

Judgments close the heart and leave you bereft of love. But you do this to yourself. As long as your heart is closed, you will never get enough love from someone else to satisfy you. You can have your judgments or you can have love. But you cannot have both.

If you have beliefs about your partner that keep your heart closed, you might as well not be with that person, as love will eventually disappear unless you move beyond those judgments and begin to affirm something more positive about your partner. Relationships cannot survive ongoing judgment. Even one judgment held by one person strongly enough can destroy a relationship.

Fortunately, since any judgment is just an idea in your own mind, you can do something about that judgment before it distorts your perception of your partner and damages your relationship irretrievably. You can catch your judgments when they form and say no to them. This is one of the secrets of those in happy relationships: The individuals don't engage in judgment, either secretly within themselves or within their relationship.

Does this sound too idealistic? Not engaging in judgment is just good emotional hygiene. Just because most people believe their judgments are useful and not harmful doesn't make them so. Judgments are useless and very harmful, and the more people who realize this, the better. If people understood this and practiced non-judgment, it would dramatically change the world you live in. There is no room in relationships for judgment because judgments leave no room for love.

Everyone has faults, or you could say lesser strengths. If you dwell on someone's weaknesses or so-called faults, then that is all you will notice. So if, for instance, you have the belief that your partner is lazy, and you feed and strengthen that belief by giving that thought your attention, you will begin to see your partner from the "he's lazy" lens and not from any other perspective. His other qualities will be overshadowed by the image that he is lazy. Your unconscious mind will look for ways to prove this belief and filter out evidence to the contrary.

The mind doesn't acknowledge the whole picture in the stories it tells about someone, and when it focuses in on a negative trait, the relationship can take a turn for the worse. What you give your attention to really matters! If you are going to focus on a belief about your partner, focus on one that enhances love. This is what people in successful relationships do. They tell positive stories about the person they are with: "He is such a wonderful person. He does so many things well. He is always considerate."

Now, he may not *always* be considerate, but when you believe this, you notice when he is considerate and filter out when he isn't, because your unconscious mind wants your beliefs to be right! Having positive beliefs about your partner supports love and helps you overlook the things you don't like. Having negative beliefs about your partner does the opposite: They undermine love and keep you focused on what you don't like. It's so important to be aware of the beliefs you have about others and to keep them positive.

Focusing on someone's positive traits is not hiding your head in the sand. Rather, doing this counteracts the mind's tendency to focus on the negative, which creates problems where there are none. The problems created by judgments and negative images of someone are illusory problems, not real ones. Judgments and negative images break apart relationships unnecessarily. Relationships are challenging enough without causing more difficulties and conflicts by holding detrimental beliefs and judgments. Watch your thoughts about your partner and be careful what you believe.

What are the stories you tell about your partner silently to yourself or out loud to your friends and to your partner? What subtle negative images do you hold of your partner in your mind's eye, and how do those images affect your relationship? This is the illusory reality you create and live in with your partner. And your partner has his or her stories and images about you that create his or her illusory reality, which your partner lives in. These illusory realities produce much unnecessary enmity, conflict, sorrow, guilt, and pain. Change your inner reality, and the outer will follow.

Chapter 5

The Past, the Future, and Now

People talk about the past and the future as if the past and future actually exist somewhere, as if they are a place you could visit, when they are nothing but ideas—in one case memories, and in the other case, fantasies. The past is completely gone, and the future you imagine never arrives. All there is, is one unfolding, ever-changing moment, which is outside of time. Some have called this "the Now," and so will I.

Time is a construct of the mind that is very useful in your day-to-day life, especially for purposes of communication. But like all mental constructs, people's understanding of time doesn't accurately reflect reality. However, because the brain processes reality in a way that creates a sense of time, you cannot escape the perception of time and everything that comes with that.

A number of illusions contribute to making time seem real. One is, as just mentioned, that the past and future feel like they exist somewhere—perhaps over the rainbow? The past and future seem real, solid. And because the past seems real, it often continues to have an impact on the ever-unfolding Now.

If the past didn't seem so real, it would leave no trace and simply be forgotten, like a boat that leaves no wake, no sign of where it has been. But your so-called past does leave a wake; it leaves memories. That is all that remains of the past, but that is something, and something that must be reckoned with.

If memories didn't carry an emotional charge and a sensory component and something else much more mysterious that makes your memories personal, your past would feel no different to you than a movie you just watched. You would be able to forget your past as easily as a movie, and there would be no residue to heal or release.

But memories have something that movies don't, which makes them personal: They are *your* movie, your story, not just a story about someone else. The same magic trick of the mind that creates a sense of being the character you are playing also gives this character a past that matters to the character—and ideas about a future.

The character you are playing not only lives in the Now, but also inside a story that includes ideas about the past and future. The character is made real by this sense of a past and future. Without a story about this character that takes place over time, the character would not exist. The character is living a story with a past and future. The me is the star of an ongoing drama, with a beginning, a middle, and an end, just like in a movie. If you take away the character's past and future, you wouldn't have a story or much of a character, because the character gains its identity from the storyline.

This is how it is meant to be. You are meant to live out a story. This story is full of sorrow, struggle, pain, and success and glory too. It is a grand story. Everyone has an amazing tale to tell of failure and triumph, love and hate, loss and new birth. You cry, you laugh, and you experience every possible experience and emotion over your many lifetimes.

And yet, the character and the story are an illusion. There is no character and there is no story—only the ever-unfolding Now, appearing as a character living out a storyline. What an excellent magic trick! That is what an illusion is, isn't it? It is something that appears to be something other than it actually is. You are here living your life, and you are also not who you think you are. You live in two different realities, an illusory one and a real one: You live as the character and you live as your essence, stripped bare of the costume and script.

Another quality of the illusion of time is that what happened in the past seems really important. The past seems not only real, but also significant. This is why people share their pasts with each other, embellishing and fleshing out each detail for all to hear. But all they are really sharing is their particular story about the past, because the past, itself, can never be shared, since it is gone. All you have are *memories* of the past, the residue, a shadow of something that happened.

That's all that is left, and that isn't much. Memories are not at all like an experience, and they do a poor job of representing an experience. All that memories are is someone's version of something that happened in the past—a story. All you have of the past is your story about it.

The memories people most cherish and dwell on are either their painful ones, in which they felt victimized, unhappy, or unsuccessful, or their happy ones, which make them feel sad because whatever made them happy is no longer happening. Such are the memories people lug around, which pass for the past. The unfortunate thing is that, by dwelling on their painful stories, people wound themselves again and again.

If memories are mostly painful, what motivates people to focus on them and share them? The answer is that stories give the character a sense of existing and definition: "I am someone who lost my mother at eight. I am someone who went into the military. I am someone who had four children." Your stories tell you and others who you are, that is, who you think you are. They give the real self, which would otherwise be unclothed, some clothing. They turn the real you, which is nameless and shapeless, into somebody.

Stories are important to the ego, which drives the character, because stories create the character. Whenever you talk about yourself, you can feel the push of the ego behind the sentences that begin with "I." To maintain the existence of the character, the ego needs to talk about itself. This is why people share their stories with others, and this is why, in their quiet moments, people think about their past. It seems important to do so, and everyone else seems to agree and to be doing the same thing. What kind of a person would you be if you didn't care about your past or other people's pasts? (Much happier!)

If the past didn't seem important, the past would be easier to forget and not so hard to heal from. These two qualities—realness and importance—give the past a dimensionality, an intensity, and a power that it does not deserve.

The past seems like much more than just a thought—a memory—even though that is all it is. It seems like more than a thought because the past is embedded not only in your mind, but also in your body. You carry your memories with you wherever you go, like belongings that you cling to, as if they were so precious—especially the painful memories.

Those are even more dear to your heart than the happy memories.

You hold your memories as treasures, and this is also part of your programming. This sense of preciousness ensures that the stories will keep being retold, which contributes so importantly to the illusion of time. So, you see, you are programmed to suffer. It can hardly be avoided, until you begin to see through the illusion cast by your programming.

The seeming importance of what happened in the past drives the character's drama forward. The past, or really the character's stories about it, causes the character to do things he or she would not do if the past didn't seem so real and important and if the stories didn't seem true. The past and, in particular, the stories about the past give the character identity and a *raison d'etre*, a reason to do what the character does.

The character is shaped by what happened in the past and the conclusions drawn about what happened. Those conclusions influence the character's present and, consequently, the character's future. The character's stories about the past determine the character's destiny along with the character's beliefs. The past and the stories related to it are imprinting, just as beliefs are imprinting. If you don't see the effect that your stories about the past are having on your current behavior, you can't be free of that behavior, just as you can't be free of the effects of your beliefs until you realize their effects.

Overcoming the power of the past and the power of your stories to determine your present and your future is largely a matter of seeing that the past is *not* real and *not* important and that it is completely gone. It is also a matter of realizing that any stories you tell about the past are incomplete and therefore false. For most, the past shadows them, shaping how they relate to others, how they feel and behave, how they see themselves, and what they envision as possible and not possible for themselves. They are controlled by a shadow—by something that isn't real.

What happened in the past is responsible for many of your beliefs, so freeing yourself from those beliefs requires seeing the truth about the past. The truth I am referring to is not the truth about what happened, although that can sometimes be valuable. But more valuable than that is realizing that the past is not important.

What happened in the past might have been important then, to that Now, but it is not important to this moment—unless you make it so. You make the past important by believing it is important and by keeping it alive through stories. Believing that the past is important becomes a self-fulfilling prophecy: When you believe that, you hold on to your memories and stories about the past, and those stories create feelings. Then that inner climate shapes your behavior and determines how you experience reality and how reality responds to you. In that way, you fulfill the prophecy that the past is important. The past can only become important if you allow it to.

If you let go of the past, you won't miss it. Memories and stories of the past do little for you or for your life except keep you living out the character's programming. Letting go of the past is not as hard as it may sound, because the past is already gone. (How can you let go of something that's gone?) All you have to let go of are your thoughts and stories about the past, which have rarely served you anyway.

Most of your thoughts and stories about the past fortify the false self. And you don't need that. You can still play the character you are meant to play but without your programming determining the script.

Instead of following your programming, you learn to improvise! In place of the script is the flow, the ever-unfolding Now. You learn to do and say what comes out of the flow to do and say.

To realize that the past is not important deeply enough to be free of it requires some inquiry into your own memories: How do you see yourself in the past? What memories have you repeatedly shared with others or dwelled on? What have you concluded from those memories, and how have those conclusions (beliefs) shaped you? Do you need those memories? How might you be different without them? Can you imagine what you would be like or how you would feel if you didn't have those memories?

Your memories, just like your beliefs, create an internal climate that determines your present moment experience. Running those memories in your mind is like running a sad movie in the background while you go about living your life. How can that be helpful? Even a happy memory running in the background only keeps you from fully experiencing the Now. A happy memory can never fulfill you or be as rich an experience as the present moment is when you give the present moment your full attention.

In reality, there is nothing but this fresh, new moment. What will you do with it? Can you approach it anew, like a baby? Can you approach the people in your life as if for the first time? Can you experience the clean, clear, empty, unbaggaged self that you really are?

To the ego, your real self is not as juicy or exciting as the character with all the character's emotions and drama. The ego wants nothing to do with reality or the real self. In each new moment, the ego attempts to pull you back into your thoughts, back into the character and its story.

If you perceive your true self through the ego's eyes, you won't be interested in the peace and love that your true self has to offer, and you won't even realize what it has to offer. You won't get to know the real you. You won't know the shining reality that exists, in which *you* exist. But it is there, waiting for you to discover it.

The future is as unreal as the past, but it is easier to see this about the future than the past. Unlike memories, no one shares their detailed fantasies of the future with others as if they believe those fantasies are real. Nevertheless, most people spend a good deal of time imagining the future, and they hold these ideas dear, as if they were real. People's dreams are important enough to them that they feel angry if their dreams are challenged and hurt if their dreams aren't also believed in and supported by those they love. Many a relationship has ended because the two people involved did not share and back each other's dreams.

There is nothing wrong with having hopes and dreams, but it is good to also be aware that you made those dreams up and that you don't actually know what will be, and to realize that you don't have much control over what will be. The ego doesn't want to admit how little control it has over the future, and it pretends to have much more control than it does.

The ego has a strange relationship with the future: It both fears the worst and imagines the best. There is no middle ground with the ego, only black and white: horrors and dreams-come-true. To the ego, the future will either be terrible or wonderful. You will be either a bag lady or a millionaire.

Just as memories from the past are programmed to feel real, important, and precious, so are fantasies of the future. One of the ways that fantasies are made to seem real and therefore believable is that they have you in them! It is *your* future. You imagine yourself in your dream house, driving your dream car, being with your dream partner. This may sound obvious, but an imagination is greatly empowered when you are part of it. Just as your memories have you at the center, so do your fantasies of the future. This makes your fantasies, like your memories, seem real, important, and precious.

This explains why people don't like their dreams dashed by others or by events. Your dreams are very personal. You are identified with your dreams. Your dreams *are* you. Who would you be without them and without your past? Exactly. That's the point. Your future and your past together create the you that you think you are. Having your dreams threatened feels like a threat to you, and so it is—a threat to your *idea* of you. Only in the illusory reality can someone else's ideas about your idea of your future threaten the idea of you. What a tangled web the illusory reality weaves!

Another way imaginations of the future are made real and believable is that they have elements in them that are already part of your reality. For instance, in your fantasy, you might still live in the same town you are in but in a more expensive neighborhood. Or you imagine that you are with the same partner, but you are traveling the world. Or you imagine that you are driving your same friends around in your new luxury car. You don't imagine yourself in someplace like Oz, where everything is unfamiliar. That would be too strange, too impossible. You would know for sure that that was a fantasy, an illusion. But if your fantasy has familiar elements, that makes it believable and seemingly possible.

Perhaps what most lends realness to a fantasy is the fact that you want it to be real: "I want it to be this way, therefore it will be." People are programmed to believe that their desires will come true. In the end, you believe you will finally get what you want. That is the happy ending everyone longs for. That is the basic fantasy: You get what you want. End of story. But in reality, there is no end of story, except perhaps death, and that is hardly the fairytale ending people are looking for.

When does your happy ending arrive? When your first child is born? Then he gets sick and has to go to the hospital. So is the happy ending when he gets better and comes home? Then he grows up and is unhappy. What if that doesn't change? Where's your happy ending? Meanwhile all the other ups and down are happening: in your career, in your marriage, in your health, in your friendships, in your finances.

Life is not a fairytale. It is also not a nightmare. It is both to the ego but neither to your real self, which is enjoying the wild rollercoaster ride called life. The ego's idea of life and reality just doesn't fit reality, and that can only cause suffering. The ego wants a happy ending, or a lot of moments that feel like a happy ending. But the ego doesn't ever get the life it wants because that would be impossible. Life is not something you order up from a menu. It doesn't comply with your wishes and commands.

Because the ego has impossible expectations, disappointment is an ongoing experience in the egoic state of consciousness. The character is constantly disappointed by life, even by very simple day-to-day experiences: Your husband brings home the wrong kind of ice cream, you break one of your favorite bowls, your daughter gets a bad report card. Every event in life is an opportunity for the ego to be disappointed, as it compares real life to its fantasy of how life could or should be.

That is the problem with fantasy and future expectations. Life doesn't live up to them, so they cause disappointment with life, when life is perfectly fine as it is. Life is unfolding exactly as it is meant to. To define this unfolding as wrong or not good enough is to tell a story about life that is simply untrue, and untrue stories, as we have seen, only make you unhappy.

Because of how you are programmed to relate to both your memories and your fantasies, you are bound to suffer. The deck is stacked against you as long as you remain in the ego's illusory world. It is a world of pain and suffering, which creates more of the same.

So how do you break out of the ego's illusory world? An illusion only needs to be seen through before it ceases to be an illusion. But the illusory reality, because it shows up in so many ways in every moment, has to be seen through again and again. Your life must become a practice of seeing through the illusion to the truth in each moment until that practice becomes automatic and no longer needed.

There is no more worthwhile endeavor than seeing through the illusion, but the will to awaken from the illusory reality has to be strong enough to take on this practice. That will comes from the Father when the time is ready in terms of your evolution. Reading this may mean you are ready. If not, then reading this is certainly making you ready. You cannot read this and not be changed by it, because once you see the truth, you cannot *not* see it. The bell cannot be unrung. Your interest in awakening has brought you this far, whether you even realize what awakening is or why you are reading this.

There is no more important practice than meditation for breaking the domination of the ego and its instrument, the voice in your head. Much has already been written about meditation and other practices that facilitate awakening by this author, so I will refer you to those writings. But please know that meditation is the key to learning to live in reality rather than in the illusory reality created by your thoughts and feelings.

The reason that meditation is the key is that it teaches you to be present to—to pay attention to—reality rather than lost in your thoughts and feelings, which create and uphold the illusory reality. Meditation brings you into the present moment, the Now. It gives you a taste of another possible way of being and living as a human. It gives you a taste of your essential self, your true nature. Once you have had enough tastes of reality to trust it, you won't want to return to your illusory reality—and you won't be able to because you are no longer ignorant of the Truth.

So here is the Truth: There is no past, there is no future, there is only the ever-unfolding Now. Whatever you call the past is the step you are in the midst of taking, and whatever you call the future is also the step you are in the midst of taking. The past and future are contained in the step you are taking *now*. The past and future do not reach beyond this one step except in your imagination. All you are ever doing is taking one step. But the experience of that step is always fresh and new, because it is as if that step is taking place in a moving river, which brings to you all manner of experience.

This river is the flow of life. Life comes to you, and you receive it, experience it, and respond to it. This is the experience of being in the Now. It is effortless, enjoyable, interesting, and wondrous. You feel as if you are moving through life, but it is more like Life is moving through you and moving you. In this way, the water of Life nourishes and sustains all life.

When you are outside the flow of life, in the desert that is the ego's reality, it feels like you have to struggle just to survive. It doesn't feel like life comes to you but like you have to make life happen through your own efforts. When you are outside the flow, the illusion is that you are pitted against life, while the flow is an experience of being beloved and held by life. In the flow, you experience life's bounty and Grace, not the ego's limitation and fear.

The Now is the experience of being held and supported by life, which is the truth. You *are* being held and supported by life. You are not separate from the life force that sustains you. You *are* this very life force. It flows through you and moves you to speak and act, whenever your speech and actions are not being coopted by the ego. You only *feel* separate. But that is the illusion. How you feel does not reflect the truth about reality. Reality is bounteous, trustworthy, and intelligent beyond imagination.

Chapter 6

A Belief That Takes You Beyond Beliefs

As mentioned earlier, some beliefs are truer than others. The more closely a belief matches reality, the truer it is. Beliefs that match reality can be useful in breaking through the spell cast by the illusory reality.

One of the most powerful beliefs for doing this is the belief "I don't know." This belief is nearly always true! Most of the time, you don't know much: You don't know what is going to happen, why something happened or is happening, or even what exactly did happen. You don't know what other people are thinking and feeling. You often don't even know what you are thinking and feeling! Any answers you think you have only cover a sliver of the truth. They are only part of the story.

There is so much that you don't know, that it is difficult to even claim that you know something. When you do claim to know something, what you think you know is usually only part of the truth, and partial truths are just not that true. For instance, you might think you know what your spouse is like. But you still don't know what it is like to be your spouse or what it is like to be your spouse here and now. Like everything else, your spouse is constantly changing, whether you are aware of that or not. How can anyone possibly know another human being, when that person doesn't even know himself or herself? And yet, people often pretend that they know others, even people they have barely met.

You could argue that you know some fact, like what day of the week it is, your name, or what the weather is like right now. But all you know is a word for the day of the week, a word for yourself, and a word for the weather. The words people use are just labels for things or for concepts created by the mind. There is actually no such thing as a week or weather; those are just useful concepts. And a name for you is not you; it is just a label. Knowing the name of something is not the same as knowing something.

What do you really know? Can you think of anything that you can say that you know? About the only thing you do know is that you exist. You are conscious of existing. But what that mystery of existence and consciousness is, you cannot begin to know.

The value of seeing how much you don't know is that it counteracts the ego's assertion that it knows so much. The illusion is largely created by pretending to know. That is what beliefs are—pretenses at knowing. You pretend to know what is best for other people, you pretend to know what is going to happen, you pretend to know what happened in the past, you pretend to know how you and others should and will behave, you pretend to know what is right and wrong, you pretend to know what other people are like and how they feel about you. The list goes on.

The ego pretends to know things it does not, cannot, and will never know. The ego does this because knowing makes it feel safe, even if that knowing is incomplete or incorrect. Pretending to know is one of the ego's survival strategies, and this strategy serves to some extent. For instance, it's useful to pretend that the sun is going to come up tomorrow, as it seems to always do. Expecting *everything* to be constantly in flux would make it difficult to function, and that would be a lie anyway, since there is a certain stability to your world. And yet, you don't really know that the sun will come up tomorrow or that you will be alive to see it. That's the truth. The truth is that you don't know even very basic things.

The trouble with pretending to know so much when you don't know—with having so many beliefs that don't match the truth—is that doing this keeps you in the illusory reality, where you will look for confirmation of those false beliefs and find them. When you believe that you can know even when you can't, you will keep turning to the mind for answers, and the mind will continue to define you and define reality for you—falsely. You will base your life and actions on pretend knowings, on beliefs, on half-truths.

The truth can only be found in reality. And the experience of being in contact with reality is that you don't know. If you aren't willing to not know, you won't want to spend time in reality. To live in reality, you have to be willing to make peace with not knowing. This is not easy for the ego. So the only way you can make peace with not knowing is to not be identified with your ego but identified with your vastness, with this great mystery that you are.

Your vastness doesn't need to know more than it needs to know. The ego wants to know so much more than it needs to know! If you knew in your heart of hearts that life is unfolding as it is meant to and that your life and every other life is in good hands, that everything you have experienced and are experiencing is what your soul intended, then would you need to know what is going to happen next? Would you need to know very much at all?

The ego thinks it needs to know so much to be safe and happy, but what if you are as safe as you need to be, as safe as your soul intends you to be? What if you could just relax and let everything be as it is? Wouldn't you be happy then? Isn't that what everyone is looking for, in all their accumulation and one-upmanship? Isn't everyone just wanting to be safe and comfortable enough to be able to relax and just *be*?

You won't find out how little you need to know if you don't spend time in reality. The ego's illusory reality is self-reinforcing. You don't discover what else is possible unless you venture out of that reality into Reality. The big leap from the illusion to reality is made possible by being willing to not know: to not know where the money will come from, to not know how you will accomplish something, to not know why something happened the way it happened, to not know what your life is going to look like or who you will be with. You have never known these things anyway. You have only been *trying* to know and pretending to know, assuming that you needed to know. But you don't.

Let Life come to you. Let Life take care of life. Leave life up to God. Your life and all life has always been up to something larger than you, something of such vast and inscrutable intelligence that it is hard to believe what is, in fact, true. You are in good hands, the best of all possible hands.

Relax and know that you do not need to know for your life to work out. And know that whatever you *do* need to know, you will, when you need to know it. Relax into not knowing. Life is much simpler that way. All you have is this ever-unfolding Now, and all you need to do is be open to fully experiencing the flow of life as it comes to meet you.

Let it wash over you, move you, speak you, dance you, love you, and be you. Peace!

About the Author

Gina Lake is a nondual spiritual teacher and the author of over twenty books about awakening to one's true nature. She is also a gifted intuitive and channel with a master's degree in Counseling Psychology and over twenty-five years' experience supporting people in their spiritual growth. In 2012, Jesus began dictating books through her. These teachings from Jesus are based on universal truth, not on any religion. Her website offers information about her books and online course, a free ebook, a blog, and audio and video recordings:

www.RadicalHappiness.com

Awakening Now Online Course

This course was created for your awakening. The methods presented are powerful companions on the path to enlightenment and true happiness. In this 100-day inner workout, you'll immerse yourself in materials, practices, guided meditations, and inquiries that will transform your consciousness. And in video webinars, you'll receive transmissions of Christ Consciousness, which are a direct current of love and healing that will help you break through to a new level of being. By the end of 100 days, you will have developed new habits and ways of being that will result in being more richly alive and present and greater joy and equanimity.

www.RadicalHappiness.com/courses

If you enjoyed this book, you might also enjoy the other two books in this trilogy by Jesus, which is also available in a single volume called **The Jesus Trilogy:**

Choice and Will: New Teachings from Jesus

Explores the complex, mysterious, and important question of who or what chooses. The question is complex because there is more than one answer. It is mysterious because our nature is mysterious and because the answer may not be what you think. The question is important because our choices shape our reality and determine our experience of it. This book was dictated to Gina Lake by Jesus.

Love and Surrender: New Teachings from Jesus

Explains the important role that surrender plays in releasing us from bondage to our conditioning into the freedom and love of our true nature. Surrender is the "miracle" that occurs when we are finally able to let go and let things be as they are. In *Love and Surrender*, Jesus, as dictated to Gina Lake, unveils this great mystery so that you can more easily live your life from a place of love, acceptance, peace, and happiness.

www.RadicalHappiness.com

More Books by Gina Lake

Available in paperback, ebook, and audiobook formats.

From Stress to Stillness: Tools for Inner Peace. Most stress is created by how we think about things. *From Stress to Stillness* will help you to examine what you are thinking and change your relationship to your thoughts so that they no longer result in stress. Drawing from the wisdom traditions, psychology, New Thought, and the author's own experience as a spiritual teacher and counselor, *From Stress to Stillness* offers many practices and suggestions that will lead to greater peace and equanimity, even in a busy and stress-filled world.

Ten Teachings for One World is a message from Mother Mary to all her beloved children on earth. The teachings are intended to bring us into closer contact with the peace and love that is our divine nature, which has the ability to transform our hearts and our world. Mother Mary's gentle wisdom will inspire and assist you in awakening to the magnificent being that you are.

Embracing the Now: Finding Peace and Happiness in What Is. The Now—this moment—is the true source of happiness and peace and the key to living a fulfilled and meaningful life. *Embracing the Now* is a collection of essays that can serve as daily reminders of the deepest truths. Full of clear insight and wisdom, *Embracing the Now* explains how the mind keeps us from being in the moment, how to move into the Now and stay there, and what living from the Now is like. It also explains how to overcome stumbling blocks to being in the Now, such as fears, doubts, misunderstandings, judgments, distrust of life, desires, and other conditioned ideas that are behind human suffering.

Radical Happiness: A Guide to Awakening provides the keys to experiencing the happiness that is ever-present and not dependent on circumstances. This happiness doesn't come from getting what you want, but from wanting what is here now. It comes from realizing that who you think you are is not who you really are. This is a radical perspective! *Radical Happiness* describes the nature of the egoic state of consciousness and how it interferes with happiness, what awakening and enlightenment are, and how to live in the world after awakening.

Choosing Love: Moving from Ego to Essence in Relationships. Having a truly meaningful relationship requires choosing love over your conditioning, that is, your ideas, fantasies, desires, images, and beliefs. *Choosing Love* describes how to move beyond conditioning, judgment, anger, romantic illusions, and differences to the experience of love and Oneness with another. It explains how to drop into the core of your Being, where Oneness and love exist, and be with others from there.

The Jesus Trilogy. In this trilogy by Jesus, are three jewels, each shining in its own way and illuminating the same truth: You are not only human but divine, and you are meant to flourish and love one another. In words that are for today, Jesus speaks intimately and directly to the reader of the secrets to peace, love, and happiness. He explains the deepest of all mysteries: who you are and how you can live as he taught long ago. The three books in *The Jesus Trilogy* were dictated to Gina Lake by Jesus and include *Choice and Will, Love and Surrender,* and *Beliefs, Emotions, and the Creation of Reality.*

All Grace: New Teachings from Jesus on the Truth About Life. Grace is the mysterious and unseen movement of God upon creation, which is motivated by love and indistinct from love. *All Grace* was given to Gina Lake by Jesus and represents his wisdom and understanding of life. It is about the magnificent and incomprehensible force behind life, which created life, sustains it, and operates within it as you and me and all of creation. *All Grace* is full of profound and life-changing truth.

In the World but Not of It: New Teachings from Jesus on Embodying the Divine: From the Introduction, by Jesus: "What I have come to teach now is that you can embody love, as I did. You can become Christ within this human life and learn to embody all that is good within you. I came to show you the beauty of your own soul and what is possible as a human. I came to show you that it is possible to be both human and divine, to be love incarnate. You are equally both. You walk with one foot in the world of form and another in the Formless. This mysterious duality within your being is what this book is about." This book is another in a series of books dictated to Gina Lake by Jesus.

Return to Essence: How to Be in the Flow and Fulfill Your Life's Purpose describes how to get into the flow and stay there and how to live life from there. Being in the flow and not being in the flow are two very different states. One is dominated by the ego-driven mind, which is the cause of suffering, while the other is the domain of Essence, the Divine within each of us. You are meant to live in the flow. The flow is the experience of Essence—your true self—as it lives life through you and fulfills its purpose for this life.

Trusting Life: Overcoming the Fear and Beliefs That Block Peace and Happiness. Fear and distrust keep us from living the life we were meant to live, and they are the greatest hurdles to seeing the truth about life—that it is good, abundant, supportive, and potentially joyous. *Trusting Life* is a deep exploration into the mystery of who we are, why we suffer, why we don't trust life, and how to become more trusting. It offers evidence that life is trustworthy and tools for overcoming the fear and beliefs that keep us from falling in love with life.

A Heroic Life: New Teachings from Jesus on the Human Journey. The hero's journey—this human life—is a search for the greatest treasure of all: the gifts of your true nature. These gifts are your birthright, but they have been hidden from you, kept from you by the dragon: the ego. These gifts are the wisdom, love, peace, courage, strength, and joy that reside at your core. A *Heroic Life* shows you how to overcome the ego's false beliefs and face the ego's fears. It provides you with both a perspective and a map to help you successfully and happily navigate life's challenges and live heroically. This book is another in a series of books dictated to Gina Lake by Jesus.

For more info, please visit the "Books" page at

RadicalHappiness.com

Printed in Great Britain
by Amazon